Needles in the Basket

Needles in the Basket

Looking at Patterns of a Woman's Life

Beppie Harrison

Deseret Book Company
Salt Lake City, Utah

Library of Congress Cataloging-in-Publication Data

Harrison, Beppie.
    Needles in the basket : patterns of a woman's life / Beppie Harrison.
        p. cm.
    ISBN 0-87579-330-4 (hardbound)
    1. Marriage — Religious aspects — Mormon Church.   2. Women — Religious life.   3. Mothers — Religious life.   4. Church of Jesus Christ of Latter-day Saints — Membership.   5. Mormon Church — Membership.   6. Spiritual life — Mormon authors.   I. Title.
BX8641.H37   1991
248.8′43 — dc20   90-21396
                                                                              CIP

Printed in the United States of America

10   9   8   7   6   5   4   3   2   1

For my mother

Contents

CHAPTER 1

Needles in the Basket

In the evening, it's nice to knit.

After dinner, when things have quieted down a little, I can pick up my needles and yarn and half-listen to television (or half-listen to my husband and the children) or sometimes just let my hands work and let my mind wander off wherever it goes. The stitches follow one after another, slipping off one needle and re-forming on the other. It would be wonderful to say that my mind gets absorbed by great and profound thoughts, but mainly that wouldn't be true. By and large, I generally spend my time thinking about fairly ordinary things because I generally spend my time doing fairly ordinary things — mostly things that had to be done before and will have to be done again. That means lots of my time is absorbed by changing sheets on the same beds, driving up and down the same driveway, pushing the shopping cart down the same aisles, picking up the same suits from the same cleaner, trying to figure out creative ways to cope with the same stupid arguments between the same children, and fixing dinner. A lot of my thinking time is spent thinking at about the same pedestrian level.

Which is okay. I sometimes think about that old Chinese curse: "May you live in interesting times." There are lots of women, otherwise much like me, who do live in very interesting times as a consequence of war and civil unrest boiling around them, and their lives are hard. Imagine never being sure what your money will buy at the market (if there is anything at the market), and having injustice not be something you think about during news broadcasts but a fact of life to live with, praying all the time that unpredictable circumstances will not, like the scorpion's tail, lash stinging in your direction. In comparison, my life is relatively safe and uninteresting. When I contemplate the alternatives, that's fine with me. Although I tend to take it for granted, it is nonetheless a blessing that I live in an orderly, predictable community—things might not be organized exactly as I'd always like, but at least my lights routinely come on when I touch a switch, and I have enough food to feed my children (even if they complain about what's available in the refrigerator), and in spite of all the talk about our violent society, I, personally, have never seen one person shoot at another in anger except on television or in the movies. Which is not to say that there is a shortage of moral issues for me to grapple with. They just present themselves as very ordinary problems.

My great-grandmother walked across the plains, fleeing the ugly face of persecution. Her trials of faith and obedience were clear-cut and memorable. My challenges are more typically episodes like deciding whether or not to trudge back across the snowblown parking lot, clutching a balky toddler, to return the extra change I was incorrectly given. (What business in the world really needs fourteen cents that badly, Satan whispers in my ear.) Or struggling to maintain control of my tongue when my husband has taken a totally unreasonable attitude and then retreats ostentatiously into important paperwork, leaving me flaming with temper. (Love one another, I'm told. Who, *him*? Why?) Hardly the kind of heroic encounters my great grandchildren will tell about with pride.

I sometimes wonder, knitting needles clicking and yarn sliding through my fingers, whether if maybe when I was voting back in that forgotten council in heaven, it all might have sounded more exciting than it's turning out to be here and now. After all, presumably we knew then that we would lose our memory of what the path of righteousness was and would have to learn it all over again down here. That might have sounded like an exciting quest, and we might not have quite anticipated that the rediscovery was more likely to involve progress through a great number of ordinary Primary and Sunday School and seminary classes (not all of which would be taught by born teachers) or maybe something as undramatic as answering the door at a not really convenient moment to find two very young men or women standing on the doorstep with a book and an inexplicably familiar message.

But maybe ordinariness like that is what we are here for. There were a few of us there in that council in heaven who turned out to be Queen Esther of Persia, or Joan of Arc, or Eliza R. Snow, or one of the other stars, but most of us aren't stars. Not now, and, most likely, not then. We don't know what our job was in the premortal existence, what it was that we were supposed to be learning. But from what we know of the plan of salvation, it seems logical that there was work for us to accomplish, and presumably we did, because we are here now. We do know our job on this earth is to be mortal, which includes such routine pitfalls as living with ordinary mortal bodies that let us down on occasion, whether it's something as transient and trivial as pimples or something permanently encumbering. We all get at least a whiff of bodily infirmity: maybe flu now, and a wonky ankle then, and nagging toothache some other day. Hardly ever do any of our ailments come at a convenient time, and sometimes our bodies let us down at the worst possible moment—which is probably part of the test.

Whatever our state of health, we have to deal with the rest of mortal life. We must cope with the strange persistence of weeds in the garden and dust kittens under the beds. We have to learn to get along with our fellow mortals: our husbands, our children and other assorted relatives, landlords, checkout clerks, and the mechanics who fix the car. We need to learn to remain composed even when organizing the Relief Society birthday social and discovering with exasperation that some of our fellow mortals might not be keeping their end up. But dealing harmoniously with these ordinary people, doing ordinary duties with sufficient grace so that we are fit to return, is precisely what we're here for.

I've often thought it would be so much easier if it was all organized for us somewhere, in precise detail. *This* is right. *That* is wrong. Then you would know what was required, and you wouldn't need to waste time making incorrect decisions. Of course, that was what Satan suggested, and on bad days when the ambiguity of earthly life seems more than ordinarily confusing, I can see precisely why a third of the hosts of heaven thought he was on to a good idea. But that wasn't the plan we chose.

What all the rest of us agreed to try was the plan that would lead us forward: to grasp the double-edged sword of free agency. We were to be free to choose, so our choice would have meaning. Inevitably, having a choice implies the ability to make a wrong choice, and one of our other jobs here on earth is to learn what to do when we've indeed chosen wrongly and how we get back on track again. Freedom to choose also means that nobody is going to provide us with a line-by-line pattern, like the knitting pattern lying on my knee, of exactly how we are to conduct our lives minute by minute. There is scripture and the counsel of the authorities and, above all, prayer, but we have to use our own intelligence and spiritual strength to find our own unique answers to our own unique challenges. The Lord has had some crisp comments to make about slothful servants who expect to have all their thinking done for them. After all, what use would we be in the hereafter if all we had learned from our experience on this earth was to do precisely as we were told?

Born amnesiac, we have to figure out and do whatever it is we were sent to accomplish, and our assignments differ not only from one individual to another but from one generation to another. We have different jobs to do. I could probably knit from the patterns left by that great-grandmother who arrived in the valley in pioneer days — assuming I could decipher the spidery handwriting and translate the terse, abbreviated directions — but what would I do with those delicately knit silk stockings now? At the time, stockings like those were the pride of the Deseret Silk Association, proudly exhibited in the Woman's Building at the great Chicago fair of 1893. "Mormon stockings" became famous. But, fine as they were, I can buy much finer (and certainly more utilitarian) down at the mall. Instead, I knit sweaters, or baby blankets, or hats. My great-grandmother made soap. I have friends who have learned to make soap, too, either as an exercise of nostalgia or as careful preparation for the unknowable future. But what makes a lot more sense for us today if we need another bar in the shower is simply to pick one up at the supermarket with the rest of the shopping. The energy my great-grandmother expended knitting her stockings and making her soap was given to me to use in different

6

ways. Sitting in my chair, knitting on my needles so like and yet so unlike hers, I wonder if I have really worked out where my energy is supposed to go.

Even the Church which is, and was, the focus of both our lives is not precisely the same. The core, made up of the unchanging eternal principles, remains as it was revealed, of course. But the Church-as-organization-in-this-world then was a struggling beleaguered group, welded together by persecution and preserved by unflagging determination. As converts entered the waters of baptism, the message to them was clear: "Come to Zion." And they came. The mountains rimming the valley enclosed the members of the Church in the safety of isolation. Once enfolded there, we dealt primarily with each other.

In time, many who were not converts also came to the valley. Drawn by our industry and prosperity, the world reached in to work with us and to live with us. Over the same years, the valley—and the Church cradled within it—reached out to the world. The Church now sprawls around the globe. New converts are encouraged to remain and build up the kingdom wherever they are. Their contributions enrich the common fabric of our lives together as brothers and sisters in the gospel, like a brightly woven ribbon with strands from a rainbow of cultures. More and more of us live far away from the central valley, looking "homeward" (even if we have never lived there) for guidance and direction but taking some of the pattern for our everyday lives from the traditions of our particular bit of the world, shared with our friends and neighbors

7

around us. Those traditions may or may not match up precisely with the traditions developed in the valley.

Which leaves us, as Latter-day Saint women, the ones who in the most ordinary, everyday ways transmit the traditions, with the interesting problem of choosing which traditions to live by and so transmit to our children. As far as the central pattern goes — the eternal, ever-constant Latter-day Saint principles — as obedient daughters of our Heavenly Father, we obviously put that pattern in the primary position in our lives. It is that pattern we want most to teach our children. But what about the rest of the design? What about what we might call the Mormon folkways, the daily embellishments that became the valley ways? What do we do about those? How do they fit with the traditions and ways of conducting our ordinary lives we find in the larger world around us? For some of us, those other variations could be the ways of our mothers and grandmothers — the ones who didn't cross the plains. For others of us, they are the ways of our neighbors and friends, which seem to fit in better with our lives in places far removed from the valley. Is there, can there be, a single pattern for all of us, daughters of God scattered across the face of this incredibly varied world he created for us?

Satan would have had such a pattern. Having rejected his plan, we are freer — and more puzzled. Like knitters with a multicolored design to knit, we have separate strands lying in our baskets. We are wives, mothers, daughters of God. Mysteriously made up of and encompassing all those roles, we are also ourselves.

8

We have the fine, clear, overall pattern into which our individual pattern must fit, and that pattern gives us a framework for the rest. We learn our individual variations by composing them, day by day and year by year. Sometimes we get it wrong, and that requires taking out and redoing. Sometimes our pattern just looks different from the pattern next to us, and we fret that maybe ours isn't right.

Some days we fret a lot. We have not only ourselves to worry about but all those others around us that we love and fuss over. We have husbands, children, parents, sisters in the gospel, and the woman next door. We may have bosses, co-workers, and in-laws who have very definite opinions about the daily decisions we make. There are times when it all seems unnecessarily complicated.

One of the nice things about knitting is that I have to think but not too much. My life isn't simple enough to live the same way. I have to make my own unique intricate pattern if it is to fit — that's my challenge and my opportunity. My great-grandmother walked across the plains, and her feet bled, and when she got to the valley her life was harsh and demanding. She shared her husband with her two sisters. She planted her own vegetables and made her own soap and cured her own bacon and knit her children their stockings — ordinary woolen ones for everyday — and sewed and mended their clothes. Her days were full of hard labor.

My life is softer, and I have leisure she never dreamed of. I also live in a much more sophisticated world. I live in the age of the automobile, which means that because I can, I am expected to fulfill obligations all over town. I take for granted the inconvenience of the telephone, which can interrupt me at any time. There are three magic boxes in my house that bring images and words from all over the world — many of them unsuitable for children and some inappropriate for people of any age — and the insistent, seductive messages of advertisers who are kissing cousins of con men. I have to defend my children at the same time I am preparing them to be adults in a world infinitely more complex even than the one I know. My husband has only one wife, but we live in a time when the permanency of marriage has become more dependent on the passing impulse of the day than on the sanctity of a promise made years ago — and members of the Church do not appear to be notably exempt from marital insecurities. The messages of the society surrounding me shout over and over that the roles of a woman I was taught to consider most integral — wife, mother, daughter of God — are at best peripheral to what should be considered first: my true self, whoever that may be.

Would my great-grandmother knit my pattern? Would I knit hers? We have not been given the choice. Her assignment was then. Mine is now. I can puzzle, wonder, even mutter to myself. But in the end, I have to pick up my own needles and start where I am.

Start here. Start now.

CHAPTER 2

Casting On

When you start out in knitting, you begin with a set of naked needles and a skein of yarn. It doesn't work quite that way with people.

A skein of yarn and empty needles are fairly neutral. You can make almost anything with them. But people start out being somebody, right from the very beginning. People who don't have much to do with newborn babies insist that they all look exactly alike, but it doesn't take long for any mother to start seeing the really remarkable differences between them. And a few minutes of standing peering through the nursery window in any hospital is all that's needed for anybody, however inexperienced, to recognize that those little bundles in neat rows are already individuals in the ways they react to their new life.

There are fussy babies and sleepy babies, irritable

babies and placid babies. It seems as if we arrive on earth at least partially programmed, with some things easy for us and other things difficult. Some of us are full of restless energy. Some of us sit. Some people — at the beginning and all through life — have a struggle holding on to a volatile temper. Patience is not their strong point. Their nature seems adapted to a swift and dramatic explosion followed almost immediately by sunny reconciliation, and they seem genuinely puzzled if their erstwhile antagonist doesn't get over it just as rapidly. Others right from the start seem to have no problem with patience, but once finally pushed too far (at any age) they smolder relentlessly. Learning to forgive, or to forget, comes hard. Amiable souls have to discover that following along just for the sake of peace occasionally gets you places you don't want to be, and natural leaders have to come to terms with the observable reality that not everybody can be organized according to your particular light.

We have different ways of perceiving the world we encounter, and out of those differences grow our talents and our blind spots. One of my daughters has always been visually oriented. As soon as she could handle a pencil she started drawing to communicate her vision of the world. I don't yet know if she will grow into the skills of an artist, but whether she does or not, she sees the world as an artist sees it. I've always paid more attention to words. I assumed that words were the meaningful way to convey experience — which meant that when my daughter was a toddler sitting on my lap while I read picture books, it never occurred to me that we were enjoying the same pages in two entirely different modes. I thought she was concentrating on the words, and she thought I was turning the pages to show her the pictures. When we are little old ladies — me a whole lot earlier, of course — I expect I'll still be verbal and she'll still be sketching on the backs of envelopes. That's just the way we came.

There are others who hear music, and some of them grow into musicians. The ones who don't nonetheless form the core of the audience musicians need, because they will always pick the melody out of the background noise. Sometimes these patterns of perception and talents are obvious right from the start. Other times they may lie dormant for decades. Think of Grandma Moses, who must have had her extraordinary capacity for artistic expression all along but who only began painting in her seventies.

We can learn and adapt and flower early or late, but do we really change? There are those who maintain that our essential natures don't really alter all that much. I have an aunt who used to declare that what her daughters and her nieces were as grown women was pretty much exactly what we'd been at two years of age. "The ones who were bossy then are managerial now, and the ones who were secretive then still are," she once told me when I was old enough to discuss my childhood on a companionable adult level. "I sometimes wonder if your mother and I made any difference at all."

But of course they did. What I am now is the result of whatever I brought to earth with me, interlined and overlaid with what my mother and my aunt taught me

13

and patterned for me. Little things: if short of time, set the dinner table first so that at least you look organized and then start working on dinner; always cook lamb with garlic; and life is more civilized if there is an interesting book to browse through in the bathroom. Big things: having married into a strongly opinionated family and having given birth to daughters who fit comfortably into that mould, my mother firmly taught us that humility included bearing in mind the remote possibility that we *might* be wrong.

Do we change? Or is it just that our life here adds layer upon layer to what we came with? Each one of those newborn babies lying side by side in the nursery gets taken home, and what goes on in that home shapes them just as much as my mother shaped me. I learned to keep peanut butter in the cupboard—it always surprises me to find it in the refrigerator at a friend's house. That's where *her* mother kept it. Are doors and windows kept open or shut? Is it fatherly to discipline and motherly to cuddle, or is it the other way around? Is sleeping late on Saturday morning delectable luxury or a clear indication of lazy disorganization? Very few of us sit down and work out these things for ourselves: mainly we take what went on in our own home as the definition of normal, unless of course we had the misfortune of growing up in a family that had problems so severe that even growing up we recognized something had gone awry.

Not only do we grow up in a home but we grow up in a culture that has a lot to do with amalgamating whoever it was we were born with whatever it is that shapes us here. There are those who claim that our whole unconscious orientation to the world is determined by what happened to be happening as we were growing up, that who we are is inevitably a product of when and where we started out. Maybe, maybe not. But if our cultural and family environment doesn't *determine* who we are, it is certainly more than a sweater we can shrug off or on at will. At the very least, it is a template—the pattern book, perhaps?—that we use to select whatever we choose to be.

Even when we're little we start that process of defining ourselves. For example, our culture may tell us what beauty is, but we each pick out our own vision of where beauty lies. I remember returning from a family outing with an older cousin of mine and his girlfriend. I must have been about thirteen at the time and was thrilled to be included with the glamorous college students. Squashed away in the back seat, I spent most of the ride home trying not to get caught staring at his girlfriend, whose short, feathery bangs curved down smoothly, perfectly, on her forehead. I can't now remember the rest of her hairstyle—except that she was wonderfully, impossibly pretty, so I assume the rest of her hair must have been as perfectly behaved as her bangs. I spent years trying to duplicate those bangs. Thinking about it now, I suspect that her hair, although it looked straight, must have had some natural wave to it. Mine most emphatically does not. Short, feathery bangs on me (unless bludgeoned into compliance by a permanent) do not curve neatly against my forehead. They stick straight out like a porch roof.

Looking at the hairstyles of the last few years, I have come to the conclusion that the porch roof effect is apparently now considered attractive in some circles. But not by me. I have long since forgotten my cousin's girlfriend's name (and since we now live across the continent from each other, it is years since I have seen even my cousin) but that girl's hair, blowing slightly in the breeze through the open car window that summer evening, remains in some undefinable way my vision of fresh, youthful beauty. Of all the images of beauty offered me by my culture as I was growing up, that was the one I chose.

I still favor that look of casual, well-kept grace. This preference of mine is inexplicable and exasperating to my daughters, who are forming their own images of loveliness, as they must, using their own methods of knitting — and their preferences seem to run to the tousled, spontaneous look. I only hope they will not latch onto porch roofs.

Inevitably, a lot of the variations in their knitting gauges will come, as mine undoubtedly also did, from the insistent world of advertising. Unfortunately, the advertisers are not just selling images of beauty. The advertisements we see and hear, and indeed the media in general, faithfully reflect back to us the whole panorama of values our culture considers relevant and persuasive. We pick and choose, of course. We have to: it is humanly impossible to do everything and see everything and buy everything that is recommended to our attention. But it is all there around us — a cacophony of voices, dramatizing one set of virtues, satirizing another set of less fashionable values, presenting chosen images as irresistibly alluring. Out of the jumble, we select the ideals and patterns that will define the women we are to become.

Fortunately, those are not the only sources we have to draw on. We watch other women and learn from them. Many of us are lucky enough to have a mother we can use as a model. There may be details we want to change here and there, but the overall shape is just about right (although we're not likely to admit that while in the turbulent rapids of adolescence). There is the Church, with its promises and exhortations and suggestions to help us forward. There are teachers, at church and elsewhere, mothers of friends, even the more distant figures we know only through news reports, or the familiar fantasies on television, who seem real because we see them week after week in our living rooms. Those fictional characters, as much as the commercials that punctuate their activities, have a message to sell: attitudes toward life, demonstrations of the ways men and women interact with each other, images of what is desirable in a woman. After all, if the thirty-second commercials are effective in persuading us that one kind of automobile is more dashing and alluring than another, it is hardly surprising that the twenty-six minutes of programming accompanying them have some influence. Whether the scriptwriters wish to take the responsibility or not, they also are teachers.

And it is when we are young and looking for our own definitions of life that we are the most vulnerable to the sales pitches. There is a wonderful, innocent self-confidence in being young, a sense that all choices are possible and that serious consequences only happen to somebody else. It's what makes youth so hopeful — and so dangerous. For one thing, the young believe they will live forever as they are now. Does anyone ever really think at eighteen that she will turn forty? The rest of mankind, maybe, but not me. As adolescents, we see all the possibilities of the world stretching endlessly before us.

Adolescents are hungry for experimentation — indeed, experimentation is their job, trying out the adult patterns they will grow into. Similarly, limiting that experimentation is the job of the adults who have responsibility for them. Experimenters learn little of value from an experiment that leads to their own destruction. The young, who by definition are immature, are not always capable of figuring out which experiments will have lethal consequences, either to their bodies or to their souls. That is what adults are for — to prevent disasters when possible, and, when not, to point out the rough road of repentance that leads back from the edge of catastrophe. One tragedy of our time is that so many voices are pointing out the attractions of temptations that skirt the edge or lie just beyond it. Another is that so many adults hesitate to warn about the hazards out of fear they will be considered spoilsports or out of their own confusion, or guilty conscience, or weariness and despair.

The young are so sure of their own view of what is real and what is fake, unclouded by the complications of life on this earth. Black is black and white is white and the grays in between can be swiftly dismissed as products of cynical adult compromise or hypocrisy. The faith of adolescents, once bestowed, has a lot in common with the unquestioning faith of children, and though some of the philosophies in which they choose to invest that faith may not have enough substance to merit their trust, the magnificent strength of the gospel is that there is enough and more to grow into. The young—and the not-so-young—can find something there to meet each one of us at any level. There is the simplicity of the message for children, the triumphant challenge for youthful seekers, the comforting matter-of-fact direction for those of us muddling through the busy middle years, and the infinite wisdom to meet us when after long years spent mastering the dailiness of life, we have slowly acquired some wisdom of our own. "The gospel is as broad as the mind that comprehends it," my mother used to tell me, and in my turn I tell the same thing to my children, when they are restless with what they see as the limitations of some of us who believe.

Maybe the headlong confidence of youth is particularly well-adapted to the circumstance that most of us are young when we make the life decisions that shape the rest of our days and have only the vaguest idea of what we are getting into. How many of us marry with any clear picture in mind of what marriage is really about? Oh, most of us have been more or less interested spectators of at least one marriage—our parents'—but everybody knows that their relationship has more to do with the pedestrian business of getting the schedule

19

straightened out of who drives whom where on Saturday morning and paying the bills than with the flush of romance and the indescribable excitement of catching the right person's eye across the room. Would we marry if we truly understood the bleak misery of being angry with the person you love best, knowing he is also angry with you? Probably not, unless we also understood the comfortable chuckles of two people who have enjoyed the same arcane jokes for years or the passion that accompanies total familiarity and intimacy. Hopefully we march into matrimony knowing more about it than we have learned from the big, or the little, screen, but we can never know it all ahead of time. That pattern comes much later in our book. We start out thinking we're knitting a potholder and years later discover it was a bedspread we were making.

The same thing is true of having children. Who ever expects that muddling confusion of emotions? We love them, we could throttle them, we adore the comforting solidness of their bodies leaning against us, we simply cannot abide their whining, we are confident they can reach the moon if they try, but our stomachs lurch as they sway uncertainly at the top of the playground slide. As they grow up themselves, our young daughters coo over the babies and dismiss as irrelevant (should we happen to mention it) that there's more to babies than cuteness. More work than they can imagine, and more reward than they would ever believe.

The curious thing is that we can't really understand any of the important parts of what it is to be a woman until we are deeply engaged in being one. It is only when you are caught up in the complexities yourself that you truly believe they exist — which is one reason our daughters look at us with the clear-eyed certainty of inexperience. The same way we, no doubt, looked at our own mothers. "Mo*ther*," we groaned, as they groan now. The answering exasperated sigh moves down the generations.

Like us, they will learn that some of the attitudes and convictions they are currently trying on for size are self-contradictory and even that some of them bear little relationship to reality once they come to experience some of that reality for themselves. They will discover that good people sometimes do, or fail to do, the most extraordinary things, and that the rules they may have chafed against exist to protect us from our own worst impulses — from which they themselves will not be exempt.

They will discover that the romantic figure with kind blue eyes whom they fell in love with and married has some provoking personal habits and was apparently brought up with an unnervingly different set of domestic assumptions. They will discover that pregnancy lasts only nine months — and a good thing, too. They will discover that bone-deep fatigue is an unavoidable part of early maternity, and very few of us are sweet tempered and cheerful when we are blurry with lack of sleep.

They will discover for themselves what we can see so clearly, looking back: that all of it up until then was just getting started on the business of living. It was taking naked needles and casting on the first row of stitches. For all of our society's focus on youth and all those beautiful unlined fresh faces that glow in our magazines and smile out from our screens, our lives as women only begin and gain resonance as we reach out and engage in life — getting in up to our elbows in the messiness and routines and delightful surprises that shape our days. Then we discover that along the way we have knit that indispensable first row, which becomes more than a succession of loops only when there is row upon row following it.

Where we start out is vital: without casting on, there is no knitting possible. But the beginning of wisdom is seeing that it is only the start. Our society may try to convince us that youth is the best time. What life shows us is that the richest times, the most beautiful, satisfactory patterns, lie still ahead.

CHAPTER 3

Knit Two Together

Men and women are different, and we can't be the first ones to have noticed.

Exactly how different we are is something people have recently spent a good deal of energy arguing about. At the moment, their conclusions range all the way from the unpopular point of view that gender is destiny to the assertive claim of some feminists that there are no significant differences between men and women that are not culturally determined, except for the obvious biological ones.

The gospel position is, as it always is, elegantly simple and commonsensical. Of course men and women are different, we are taught. Our gender identity was, is, and will be a part of what we are. The possession of gender roles is not a peculiarity of our life on this particular earth. It is simply a fact of existence. Females are females, to accomplish certain tasks, and males are males, to accomplish others.

So far, the gospel and the traditional philosophy of many societies sound pretty much alike. Where those philosophies differ from the gospel is where they go on to conclude that one set of tasks is more important, or more powerful, or more generally worthwhile than the other set, and therefore the doers of the one set of tasks have the God-given right to dominate and be served by the doers of the other set of tasks. It's at that point that the feminists begin yelling, and we in the Church politely part company with the traditionalists.

We agree that there are differences. In the broadest sense, men have been given the responsibility of the outside world. Through the priesthood, men have the responsibility of overseeing the day-to-day organization of the Church. As husbands and fathers, they have the responsibility of directing and providing for their families. In the same sense, women have been given the responsibility for the inside world. We are the keepers of relationships and have the responsibility of the home. We are the childbearers and nurturers and the earliest teachers of our children. Our attitudes establish the emotional tenor of the places we and our families live—which sounds splendid in the abstract, but can be a pain in the particular when you are having a bad day and feel crabby and disagreeable and the entire family with a single impulse gazes into the mirror of your mood and one and all become equally crabby and disagreeable. On the other hand, shouldering the Sunday-to-Sunday organizational responsibilities of the wards and stakes of Zion and enduring countless meetings, some of which are efficient and to the point and a lot of which aren't, is not necessarily a barrel of fun all the time, either. Different responsibilities, with different pluses and minuses, but the important point is that in God's plan for us, neither is more important than the other. You have a whole grasp of the plan only when the two halves are combined, as proud and equal partners.

Which is how we arrive at the interesting arrangement we call matrimony, in which two individuals who are different by nature (as we understand it) and cultural training (which is absolutely obvious if you look around) attempt to create a shared life in which they live in the closest possible emotional, spiritual, financial, and physical intimacy. No wonder so many of us discover potholes in our road to bliss and harmony! It's a good thing that the system is fueled by love, which gives the whole process its unique element of purest delight as well as exasperation and befuddlement.

Knitting is a whole lot simpler. You simply take two stitches, which look very much alike, and knit them together — presto, you have the beginning of a pattern. In the same way, a man and a woman, when they decide to marry, join together to start a pattern. But whereas what the finished knit item is going to be is precisely defined and illustrated in the knitting book, in the real-life world of marriage, the man and woman most closely involved probably have no idea whatever of what their eventual pattern is going to look like — or even more, feel like. When we start out, few of us imagine that there are ever going to be any changes from the way we are right now.

What *do* we expect when we marry? A lot depends, I suppose, on how young we are. If a bride is young and full of ideals (but inexperienced in calculating the price she will have to pay for maintaining them), and particularly if she grew up in a home where her parents were making a reasonable success of their own marriage, the most obvious thing to assume is that marriage with someone she loves is easy. It's like playing house with a beloved playmate who makes her pulse race, with nobody to step in to send them both home or dictate "so far and no farther." And she will do all the things her mother did to please her father, and they will live happily forever after. Except maybe the things her mother did will drive her husband absolutely wild, since he arrived with a different agenda and marital expectations, and instead of two lovers purring with pleasure there are suddenly two young unhappy kids staring at each other with defiant bewilderment. Nobody expects that kind of forlorn impasse, but it happens to almost all of us over issues major or minor. It doesn't mean the marriage is over or doomed to the doldrums or that the bride and groom have fallen out of love with each other. It just means they have stopped dreaming and now have to cope with life.

For those who are older or have less happy experiences with the marriages of others, the scenario is apt to be different only in that our bride is less surprised. If she is older, she is likely to have a somewhat more developed sense of herself, which may prevent her from concluding instantly that the whole thing is entirely his fault or entirely hers. To the extent that greater maturity and wider experience encourage balance and a more sensible, less emotional approach to problems, it is unquestionably an advantage. If, however, our bride chooses to see the first difficulties in her marriage as validation of her observations that marriage is too often a disappointing, embittered arrangement, she may well be launched on a self-fulfilling prophecy and, perhaps, tragically give up at the very beginning rather than settle down to the unromantic job of building a functioning relationship.

So many of our first disagreements are really just defining what those functioning relationships are going to be like! Obviously, a lot of that work can be done harmoniously—and there are couples who seem to glide through the initial stages—but most of us find that no matter how much we are really in love, we get seriously annoyed with each other while we're settling down to being everyday married.

Well do I remember a simmering series of rows with my brand-new husband which on the face of it concerned how warm we were going to keep the apartment, whether Saturday morning was going to be spent housecleaning, and what happened when wet glasses were set down on the glass-topped table in the living room. Looking back on it, I can see that what we were really doing was establishing (a) our style of arguing: neither of us feels comfortable with shouting at the other, so we tend to communicate with icy glares and very carefully modulated tones of voice, a technique which over the years we have become so proficient at that we can conduct a spirited quarrel during which an outsider would probably be only vaguely aware that anything was wrong—but by golly *we* know what's going on; (b) that under normal circumstances I am the one to decide what level of tidiness is going to be maintained, but then I am also the one to maintain it; and (c) that one high priority will be spending leisure time together, even if that means that household chores get neglected. At times this means I wonder gloomily whether our neighbors are going to organize a petition about the state of our yard, but we have had some very pleasant Saturdays together, sometimes just the two of us and sometimes the whole family. None of these are conclusions I would necessarily urge on anyone else, but they are our conclusions, and, reasonable or not, they suit us. Maybe there was a way to come to those conclusions with less emotional wear and tear in the early stages, but I don't think we really understood that we needed to work out that kind of thing in the early stages. We just blithely assumed those arrangements fell into place of their own accord, and when they didn't, we crashed into each other and reacted indignantly.

Every couple has to work out its own arrangements. One troublesome element of present-day life—heightened by the chorus of voices trying to offer advice on how virtually any relationship can and should be handled—is the prevalent idea that there is one pattern for successful marriage: one kind of perfect wife, one kind of sterling husband. Of course, not everybody agrees on what kind that is. There are those who hit

28

the best-seller lists by decreeing that the perfect wife greets her husband at the door wrapped in see-through plastic wrap, and those who feel that in the long term cozier domestic qualities are more to the point. There are traditionalists who maintain that the sterling husband is strong and stalwart, a tower of strength in all circumstances, and trendier souls who advocate that the ideal is a sensitive husband who is as comfortable as a woman with communicating feelings and is willing to share the grunt work of sorting dirty laundry and changing the baby.

The fact is that real people seldom fit into anybody's arbitrary pattern. Real people have idiosyncrasies and glitches and virtues and awkward shortcomings, and no matter how hard we may try to reach the ideal, on the days when the plumbing backs up and the baby has an earache and the left rear tire goes flat and the mail is misdelivered, we are likely to care less about having or being the perfect marriage partner than we care about having someone around who will help get us out of the mess, even if our style of getting out of messes includes being less than totally charming to each other for the time being. Perfect people don't marry each other. Undeniably imperfect people do, and the colliding and stumbling of everyday marriage is one of the ways we are polished into perfection. But that's where we get to, not what we start with.

What we start with is two people who are completely unique separately and who will form a completely unique union. Once we get away from theory (and look beyond the shelf of self-help books), it is perfectly obvious from the most casual observation of reasonably successful marriages that there are as many ways to have one as there are marriages.

There are husbands who notice everything that goes on in the home, and husbands who seem to wander in and out in a benevolent fog and focus only when something really remarkable happens (such as stepping on the cat's tail or discovering that there is really no more milk in the fridge). There are wives who do the bills, and wives who get an allowance. There are couples who argue noisily and make up enthusiastically, and couples who are pointedly silent at each other and ooze into reconciliation. There are couples in which he does the wage earning (all of it) and she does the housekeeping (all of it). There are more and more couples in which she does some wage earning and he does some housekeeping, although most surveys suggest that typically she does more wage earning than he does housekeeping. There are couples who read together, and couples who fish together, and couples who do their own things at opposite sides of the family room but look up and beam companionably at each other.

However different the styles, there seem to be lessons that we all have to learn, and marriage seems to be a remarkably efficient schoolmaster. We all have to learn patience, for example. Rome was not built in a day, as they say, and neither was a marriage. Nor is a spouse, with all the good will in the world, going to be able to abandon an irritating habit or learned pattern of response overnight, no matter how sincerely you have both agreed that it has to be abandoned. Some may never be, which brings us to the second lesson we all have to learn: tolerance.

During our courtships, most of us are intoxicated by our similarities — that there really is one other person who feels *exactly* as we do. Marriage is the arena in which we work out our differences and how they are going to fit together and face the fact that some of them are going to involve lifelong accommodation. He loves sports. In the early flush of love, being anywhere with him was marvelous, even shivering in the bleachers. Once you can be together with him twenty-four hours a day, you discover you have a pronounced preference for being together somewhere that is dry and warm, and you couldn't care less what those sweaty men running around on the field are doing, not even if one of them is your beloved.

Or perhaps you discover that your mother-in-law is going to play a larger part in your marriage than you ever imagined. She's a fine woman (or maybe she isn't) and now that she's widowed, it is only reasonable that the gentleness and compassion that makes your husband so lovable means that he refuses to exclude her, and you're prepared to see more of her but the more you see of her, the more irritating she becomes and the more shrewish you feel. But when you try to explain it to him, you can't bear the expression of puzzled disappointment in his eyes. Or maybe it's you and *your* mother.

Or maybe one of you has a need for financial security that feels to the other like miserliness, which may be adjusted over time but never overcome. Or maybe it's—but there are hundreds and thousands of possibilities. I very much doubt that any woman who has been married more than six months could not produce a short list of qualities her husband possesses that she wishes in her deepest heart of hearts might be different, but in view of all his other splendid qualities she is prepared to put up with them. Her husband could unquestionably produce a corresponding list. That's what most of the everyday work of marriage is all about: coming to agreement on large issues and learning tolerance on the minor ones. And nobody but the two who are actually in the marriage can decide which issues fall in which category.

Above all, we all have to learn unselfishness, a lesson that is raised to the virtuoso level when we add children to the blend. Before my husband and I were married, my bishop told us that often in marriage you need love most when you deserve it least and a large part of unselfishness in marriage seems to involve leaving *deserve* out of the equation altogether. Marriage should be 50/50, we are told: a nice comforting proportion. The trouble is that 50/50 overall usually means 20/80 and 60/40 and even 100/0 from time to time. During bad spells, it can feel like 100/0 a lot of the time. Obviously, no marriage is going to survive in a healthy condition if it is 100/0 or even 90/10 most of the time, but our memories tend to fix on the periods when our contribution was measurably greater much oftener than we remember the times when our husbands were nobly enduring us. Often, unselfishness demands that we simply say, "I will continue to love you because I love you," whether or not there is any logical reason why either one should love the other right then.

Unfortunately, that is not a position that carries a lot of societal support at the moment. The more popular attitude appears to hold that hanging in there with a marriage that's having difficulties shows a lack of gumption and is probably psychologically unhealthy. Sometimes when I am standing in the checkout line absentmindedly staring at the scandal sheet display or when I hear the hot news that yet another couple of my acquaintance is splitting up, I get the feeling that marriages are now unraveled in the same matter-of-fact way that you would unravel a stretch of knitting because it looked bumpier than you'd like. It used to be that divorce was unthinkable, and a divorced man or woman carried the heavy burden of social ostracism. Divorce was taken as an indication of personal failure. That attitude is now seldom found outside the Church at all and only occasionally inside it. The good side of the new permissiveness is that partners are no longer confined by social pressure to a wretchedly miserable marriage — and let's be realistic. There *are* wretchedly miserable marriages, and divorce can be a merciful solution for everyone concerned, especially the children. The bad side of having divorce be an easily accessible option is that a lot of marriages that could have been workable if both partners had hung around to work on them now fall apart because there is a great big escape hatch and it looks a lot simpler to try something else instead.

One of the great strengths of marriage is its permanence. If it is taken as a given that the two of you are going to be together forever, it is worth putting up with one unsatisfactory part of the relationship because you are working on another—you have plenty of time to get around to both. If you are evaluating your marriage on a day-to-day basis, everything pretty much has to be in line all the time. If we take our attitudes from what we hear on television and read in the gossip magazines, then if it isn't working, hey, why bother? It seems kind of masochistic to put up with that 70/30 or 60/40 stuff, much less the 100/0. We don't think about it as an issue of unselfishness. All the pop psychology encourages us to make our evaluations on what they present as the practical angle: what's good for you now. Sticking around when things are tough, in that light, is plain stupid. "Are you going to let him get away with *that?*" the voices challenge you.

The problem for those of us who are willing to hang in there and work to get through the rough patch is that the impermanence of modern marriage is there, all around us. Even if you are determined not to use it lightly, you know the way out is there—and you know your husband knows it too. Maybe, in an ironic way, it was easier back in the hard days when marriages were only dissolved in cases of utter desperation. The walls held you in, true, but they held you in together, and you both had to stay and fight it out. And sometimes you discovered what you were fighting about were mere trivialities, just as sometimes now-divorced couples look back at what precipitated the final collapse and regret that they didn't just give it one more try.

Not all the marriages that are dissolving around us in such depressing numbers fall apart because of trivialities. Reasons for getting divorced are, after all, almost as individual as the reasons for staying married. In these days of redefinition of a woman's role, some among us come to grief because of the disparities between the Latter-day Saint view of the interlocking relationship between men and women and the present fashion outside the Church in which women are applauded for putting their own fulfillment ahead of everything else. To put your own ambition on the back burner, even temporarily, is castigated as hollow martyrdom. A woman should be free to be whatever she can be, the argument goes, and if her husband can't or won't accept that, that's tough. When you're having problems figuring out how to make room for what you want to be in your marriage, the voices urging you to keep your eyes fixed on your own goals can be tempting sirens. The plain fact is that unselfishness isn't easy. Deciding to wait to do your own thing and help your husband do his instead isn't a once-and-for-all decision. It has to be made day after day, and when there are a lot of people around you who clearly think you're nuts, that doesn't make it any easier. We were never promised a world in which all the frustrations would be conveniently removed as soon as we have embarked on an unselfish course. (It often feels as if they get even worse!) It is hardly surprising that some sisters figure it's not worth it and bail out to try their own wings. Some marriages creak with the strain and survive, and some marriages don't.

Even for the women who choose to embrace the traditional role of wife, there are pitfalls. There is a temptation for some Latter-day Saint women (and, quite honestly, some men as well) to believe that patriarchal authority in the home implies a master/serf relationship in the marriage, and since few women are really happy as serfs, this attitude leads inevitably to discontent with the self, the marriage, and, unfortunately, sometimes with the Church. The truth is, there is nothing in the prerogatives or responsibilities of the priesthood that entitles a man to have his socks picked up off the floor. If you don't want to do it, that's a gripe for you to work out with your husband, not with the Church. There are a lot of sensible, bright women (Latter-day Saint and otherwise) who do pick up the socks. But that's because they choose to do so. They aren't obliged to do it. Picking up the socks (if your husband happens to be the kind who drops them instead of neatly placing them in the hamper) has its advantages. For one thing, it keeps the bedroom tidy. Not arguing about it keeps your powder dry for more important engagements — working out with whose family you will spend Christmas or Thanksgiving, for example. Or sometimes you may be picking up the socks as a way of cherishing him because of all the private ways he cherishes you.

But marriage isn't always tit for tat. When we are young and our concept of relationships still immature, everything has to be evaluated as fair or not, as our children endlessly remind us. "It isn't fair!" is the clarion cry of the offended party. Theoretically, we grow up and look at things with a longer perspective. But when we consider how childish we can be about such crucial marital issues as who pulled more covers over to which side or who ought to go out and get the mail out of the mailbox, it is hardly surprising that we find ourselves muttering "It's not fair" about other problems.

Well, it may not be fair, but it seems to be true that women (in general) are more sensitive than men (in general) to the subtleties of maintaining a relationship. There are those who claim we had to learn those skills because we have always been in the subordinate position and it behooves the prisoner to learn to interpret the moods of the jailer. Well, maybe. But however it came about, women seem to be the ones who know what's happening in the marriage. (Divorce lawyers are all too familiar with the sad stories of husbands who had absolutely no idea that their wives were discontented before the day they walked out.) Looking after the marriage relationship itself has always been women's work. We are the talkers, the soothers, the ones who notice tones of voice, the significance of expressions, the body language indicating happiness or annoyance or any of the way stations in between. One of the things that is undeniably hard on marriage today is the reality that we are all time-poor. We are all, both husbands and wives, so locked into outside activities, whether paid or not, that too often nobody has the time to tend the marriage. Some men can't, or don't, and some women carrying household responsibilities and mother responsibilities and Church responsibilities and job responsibilities are understandably just plain too tired to see those things any more, and some women have bought into the "Why me? It isn't fair" argument and refuse to play.

Looked at in me-terms, it doesn't make sense. Why should it be up to the woman to nurture the marriage? Why shouldn't men be brought up to be as perceptive and sensitive as women? (Possibly some improvement along that line would be a splendid thing under any circumstances and we should go to work on our sons, but we might be starting a bit late in the day for our husbands.) Practically speaking, whether on the short-term or the eternal basis, there is one pertinent question: if you don't tend your marriage, who will? How much do you want that marriage to endure? Would you rather be mathematically fair and insist he does his part right now, or would you rather do a bit more giving and a bit less taking and build the kind of relationship that lasts for decades (and probably balances a whole lot better over the long run)? Do you want to have a marriage that warms and shelters your mutual old age and goes forward into eternity?

Love helps. It is no accident that the primary commandment Christ gave us was to love one another. It's unfortunate that in talking about marriage we always seem to concentrate on the difficulties and not on the enjoyments. Love is fun. Love is splendid, and love doesn't stay exactly the same from day to day and week to week. One of the comforts of marriage is discovering that you can be reasonably fond of each other in February and passionately in love in July and get along okay in September and have the passion flare back up for no good reason to warm you in a bleak and windy November. One of the scary parts of early marriage is discovering that the first wild enthusiasm of fresh love doesn't last, and one of the reassuring parts is sticking around to discover that the mature warmth of intimacy does, and it goes on through all the fluctuations in your enthusiasm about each other. We don't admit often enough that there are pleasures in realizing on an absolutely routine Tuesday that you are as excited to see him walk through the door as you were the first week you were married. Or that there is special felicity in knowing everything about each other's bodies, or that one of the particular delights of being a human being is retaining the capacity to surprise each other, even after years and years of living side by side. Making each other laugh gets better as your shared vocabulary grows deeper and more resonant, and there is nothing comparable to the knowledge that he has seen you at your best and at your absolute worst and still considers the whole package worth keeping at his side.

None of those strengths shows up well in a half-hour sitcom or even in a full-length movie. One of the elements that made *On Golden Pond* so popular with audiences was that it managed to show that kind of relationship successfully. New love is usually a lot more interesting to an audience because what's going on is clearly visible to bystanders. Almost universally we underestimate our parents' marriage (unless they and we live long enough to look at each other with the distance of adulthood) because the most important part of it is private and ripples away quietly under the surface. We are geared to rapid action and the visible drama of separation and reunion and dancing until dawn. Twenty years later dancing until dawn still might be fine (if you can sleep late the next morning and have been taking your vitamins), but there is a lot to be said for sitting quietly on the stand in the full view of the congregation and listening to your husband speaking at your son's missionary farewell—and little of that could you ever hope to explain to those shiny-eyed girls sitting with their parents.

None of that richness comes along without the everyday work of tending a marriage, and when you consider the rewards, the whole question of what's fair and who has done the most of it becomes much less important. When you've mellowed from the excitement of exploration through the ordinary routines of working out budgets and dishing out casseroles into the comfort of loving intimacy, spent long years of flexing around each other, shaping your bulges to fit his hollows and vice versa, you've gone on a long journey that nobody else could ever come close to evaluating. To give yourself to that kind of marriage means that each of you will inevitably be a part of what the other person grows into being. After twenty or thirty years or more of living together, the long interplay between you will mean that in the most literal sense you would both be different people if you had never married each other. If that's what you're going for, a bit of sock-picking-up

40

(if that's what it is at your house) or sticking it out through the 100/0 or 90/10 patches is neither here or there.

The way you knit your two together probably wouldn't work next door, or for your Relief Society president (unless you *are* your Relief Society president), or for your kid sister. They have to figure out their own way of knitting. Even your method is almost certainly not what you thought it would be in the beginning. For one thing, you didn't know nearly as much about the boy who turned into your husband as you do now, and for another, you sure didn't know that much about you. Nor could you have predicted what would happen when the pair of you were buffeted by outside circumstances in a world where few of us live under golden umbrellas and bad things certainly do happen to good people.

Marriage isn't easy, and if it is to play its part in preparing us to move along to a life in which even more will be expected of us, I don't see how it ever could be easy. Getting along with each other and simultaneously progressing in the same direction is the most complicated job any of us will undertake. Compared to that, raising children is a part-time job. They grow up and go out and take responsibility for themselves; husbands and wives have to go on getting along as working partners for the rest of our lives here and hereafter. Marriage takes all the possibilities and problems of all the rest of human relationships and compresses them into a nutshell. You respect and obey your parents, and there is an element of that in your

41

relationship with your husband. You tend and nurture your children, and when you or your husband are ill or feeling defeated, you tend and nurture each other. You have the pleasures of companionable equality with your friends, and you have exactly the same relationship in your marriage.

When you knit two together with yarn and knitting needles, you do it once only with each set of stitches. When a woman and a man are knit together in marriage, the knitting together becomes a continuous process that is repeated daily in a thousand different ways. When two stitches are knit together, they lose their identity and become a single combined stitch. With marriage, the husband and wife also gain a new identity as part of a partnership, but when the marriage is working well, they each retain their own identity as well, enhanced and embellished by the interplay between them.

There are those in the world who won't see that. Those are the ones who insist on seeing marriage as a relationship in which a woman's identity is necessarily absorbed into that of her husband and his family. Look at the names, they say. Why should it be the woman who gives up her name and becomes Mrs. Somebodyelse? Look at the job, which involves doing the grubbiest, least dignified services imaginable. Do husbands do that kind of stuff? Not very many of them. Not very often.

Well, the name business bothers some people and doesn't bother others. As the new legion of children of divorce who wind up in families with a miscellany of surnames can testify, it's a lot easier when a whole family has the same name—and since we see our husbands and fathers as the head of their households, it's only logical the name should be theirs. Perhaps the Hispanic cultures, which traditionally carry on both the maternal and the paternal surnames, have it about right. But is that *important?* A rose by any other name, and so forth. You can always carry on your family name as your children's middle name: it will certainly make your descendants' genealogy a bit easier.

It is also true that being a wife and mother is likely to include some fairly gross moments. Few of us would classify as the high points of our family experience the times when we have to clean up after somebody who has just thrown up; but Jesus washed the feet of his disciples, which in those days of bare feet and minimal sanitation must not have been markedly more appetizing. What he was teaching us was that whatever we do, if we do it with love, has dignity and importance. Among all the other things marriage gives us is the unavoidable opportunity for service. It is only in service that we discover who our truest selves are, that we gain our greatest dignity, whether the service is something as visible and gratifying as putting together a flawless company dinner for his important guests, or something as humble and ordinary as making sure that his socks match and there's a clean shirt available, morning after morning and year after year. Sometimes we serve the men we love; sometimes—and we mustn't let even the loudest cynics encourage us to forget it—the men we love serve us.

Marriage is too complicated to fit into any simplified formulation. It doesn't always work, but we have been given the promise that it can, that we can — that men and women, different as they are, are meant to give themselves wholly to each other to build a relationship of such depth and profundity that it can't develop any other way. Marriage is meant to be a relationship that transcends the whole issue of equality, a relationship in which one and one add up to something greater than the sum of the parts. It might not always be easy, but there's no other way to get to where we want to go. And if we get it right, the potential is breathtaking.

Knit two together? Absolutely. Day after day after day. And then again the day after that.

CHAPTER 4

Cables, Bobbles, and Other Flourishes

Most knitters, once they get the hang of plain knitting, experiment with more challenging patterns. In a similar way, most of us go on from marriage to add the greater complication of childraising. Some of us discover we are producing a new bobble, so to speak, as a matter of course; others of us discover that the process, simple in theory, takes a bit more effort to get on track. But however it happens, for most of us it does happen. We take on the job of watching over a vulnerable spirit freshly arrived in the world with excitement, some anxiety, and (particularly when it's our first go at parenting) transcendent naïveté. Not only do we not know how to cope with many of the challenges but we don't even imagine they exist.

At the beginning, most often, it's like falling in love. All you can see is the incredibly finely crafted baby lying in your arms, fingernails and delicately curved ears so small and so perfect, a warm bundle stirring sleepily or wide eyes studying your face with precocious intensity. Anyone can tell you beforehand that you will love your child; no one can begin to tell you how that feels. As with marriage, you find out about the complications later on.

I know I'm not the only one to wonder wistfully on bad days why I ever thought having children was such a great idea. Oh, the instructions "to replenish the earth" sound perfectly reasonable in Relief Society and sacrament meeting (unless your two older ones happen to be shoving each other at the time and the baby has just crawled across your lap for the forty-second consecutive time). And it is also true that children are wonderful. All the soppy poems and saccharine art have it just about right: there *is* nothing like the feel of a child slipping a small hand into yours or the trusting openness of a child's face looking up at you. It's the other times that get to you. For instance, that exhausting, disorganized time just before dinner when the day is winding down and they are tired and hungry and you have been a good mother all day long and are getting pretty weary yourself. That's when they hang on your legs and whine while you are cooking and then get in your way, insisting on your attention while you are trying to get the food out of the pans and onto the table before anything burns or goes cold or both. That's when I find myself wondering why the young of the race can't be raised somewhere else by robots who are incapable of fatigue or irritation.

It happens to be my personal theory that the logic behind the commandment that we marry first and then have children is that we need marriage for the preliminary training in involuntary unselfishness. Mothering is the intensive post-graduate level. Whether we bargained for it or not, whether we had any idea of what we were getting into, we are forced into growth, turning ourselves outward day after day to meet the needs of our children, getting around to our own personal priorities later if at all. When we first take those soft crumpled babies in our arms, do we have any presentiment of how much selflessness we are going to have to learn?

Pregnancy is sometimes the cold-shower introduction to the new order of precedence. I remember it well. I discovered I was pregnant with my first child in the late spring. Late spring also happens to be the one time of year when I am afflicted with hay fever, and just after my pregnancy was confirmed, I began sneezing and my nose dripped morosely and continually. Of course there was absolutely nothing I could do about it. The previous year I had been given a medicine that made spring bearable, but the doctor could not promise me with certainty that it would be safe for the baby (who was of course in the most vulnerable stages of early development), so I had no choice. No reasonable choice. I was already feeling more tired than I had ever thought people got, nausea turned me bright green in the morning and pale green the rest of the day, and now along with the sneezes, the back of my throat itched, and as a result of continual blowing, my nose was chapped and sore as well as damp and sticky. I did

47

not feel beautiful. I opened the medicine cabinet and stared moodily at the bottle of pills that would at least relieve the hay fever and knew I could not take them. Because of the baby.

Spring passed, but the new priority did not. Because of the baby I drank quantities of milk and orange juice and took iron pills that made me constipated. Because of the baby I watched my diet and my weight and spent unreasonable amounts of time sitting in the obstetrician's waiting room clutching specimen bottles. I underwent the indignity of examinations and worried about my blood pressure. Because of the baby I went to bed early at night (although that was no great sacrifice in the early months and towards the end — I would quite contentedly have gone to bed at eleven in the morning). Because of the baby my friendly familiar body changed its whole shape to accommodate her increasing bulk, and my pantyhose wouldn't stay up and my shirts wouldn't stay down. My unfortunate stomach was apparently shoved up next to my throat, and every time I lay down I tasted everything I'd eaten for the last several hours. All because of the baby. And I had an easy, straightforward pregnancy! Even so, I leaned against my husband and had rebellious moments when I felt as if I had changed from being a person into being a host for an anonymous parasite.

Those were the down times. There were the others, too. Because of the baby I was alight with anticipation and kept stopping to feel her shift around — delicate flutters at first but eventually great thumping movements, and occasionally we had the delighted excitement of seeing the identifiable bulge of a knee or elbow. I made lazy, elaborate plans for the new life we would have together, this baby, her father, and me. Only, of course, then I had to take into consideration the possibility that she might be a he, and so there were all the alternative plans for a son, which were made redundant when she turned out to be my daughter but could be retrieved years later when her brother was born. I inspected all other babies with new attention and counted the days until mine would be born, partly because it meant deliverance from pregnancy (quite literally), but mainly because I could hardly wait to have her with me and see her face and really begin mothering. In spite of my passing spasms of resentment, I still didn't recognize that I was already turning into a mother.

Then she was born, and I loved her wholly, fiercely, adoringly. I still do.

It was true that the end of pregnancy taught me several lessons. We all learn them. The first was that they don't call it labor for nothing. Having a baby may be exhilarating or shattering, but either way it's a whole lot of work. The second, which I learned shortly after the hospital handed her over to us for care and keeping, was that she was going to do more to determine my schedule than I was likely to do to determine hers. My command of my own time was abruptly a wistful memory. The third was that there is more to be done with a baby than holding her on your lap and making loving noises. There is feeding, bathing, laundering, putting things away, getting things out, trying to straighten the house, and all of it is continually interrupted.

Mothers are *always* interrupted. Long after the children have left the cuddly baby stage, they go on interrupting you. They interrupt your work, your conversations, your thoughts. Even after they grow up, the process seems to go on: looking at those just ahead of me on the child-raising timetable, I observe that their adult children still interrupt, exploding in and out of their parents' lives at their own convenience. It occurs to me that I still explode in and out of my mother's.

Nor is it just a matter of perpetually trying to remember what you were in the middle of when that child demanded attention. The cold reality is that we spend years doing things we don't particularly want to do when we don't want to do them. Somewhere there may be a woman who just loves getting up at 3:50 A.M. to cope with the shrieking infant she last saw at 2:38, but I haven't met her. Most of us crawl out of our lovely warm horizontal beds reluctantly and return thankfully. As one of my daughters once observed pensively when her baby brother was going through a prolonged teething period that appeared to bother him mainly between midnight and 3 A.M.: it's a good thing babies are cute. She spoke wisely. One of the truths about motherhood we all discover is that we can positively dislike our children when we are jolted out of sleep to go tend to them, and another is that once we get to their bedside we can be bowled over by the surge of love we feel for the small, soft, hopelessly dependent human beings nuzzling against our warm and sleepy bodies. In those moments we learn the lesson the Lord means us to learn about love and service: the deeper the space we hollow out by unselfish service to others, the greater the area available to be filled with the love that is our mortal link with divinity. As women, as mothers, we're lucky. We get to learn that whether we mean to or not.

From that lesson we go on to another that we began with our husbands and have to extend and amplify with our children. With our husbands we called it tolerance: we learn to cope lovingly with what we can't change. It can be a surprise to discover that there are also things about our children we can't change. They arrive, as we did, with individual temperaments that might mesh and blend with our own or might not. With our husbands, we're dealing with adults: we can fight fair. Our children are so young and so vulnerable, and what we say to them about themselves forms such a large part of what they think about themselves. What we have to learn with them is forbearance and self-control.

Coping with a growing child, teaching him what he has to learn to fit into the world and yet not be a part of it, is a long and sometimes excruciating experience. You learn a great deal about each other in the process. You learn about the strengths and weaknesses of the child, and sometimes your child learns more than you would like either of you to know about yours. Sometimes your individual strengths interlock, and you can offer that child exactly the right combination of correction and support. Sometimes weaknesses challenge weaknesses. Maybe the child who needs patience most has the trick of exasperating you almost past endurance. Maybe the child with a flaring temper that needs control repeatedly kindles your own temper, and the temptation to let fly is almost irresistible. When you are caught up in confrontation — particularly when it is simply a different variation on the same confrontation you have been caught up in one way or another with that child over and over — it can be a miserable experience. Because you care so deeply about your children, you can't shrug the unhappiness off. Whether you are at peace or at loggerheads, the two of you are joined together. This is the child your Heavenly Father has sent to you, and one way or another, the two of you have to cope with each other. Hard as it may be sometimes to figure out, there is a reason the two of you were given to each other. You have lessons to teach each other, and once you've weathered the process, you will each be more of what your Heavenly Father knows you are capable of being.

Self-control is not a lesson we learn when everything is going smoothly. Forbearance is not a skill we develop when everything around us is pleasing. The peaceful, happy times here on earth certainly give us the taste for the more serene life to follow when we shall have joy as a matter of course, but the bumpier stretches between those oases are where we are ground and polished into something a little closer to the perfection we will need to get there. Perhaps there are mothers who have only the peaceful, happy times with their children and learn from conflict elsewhere, but most of us find that our struggles with our children become one of the primary polishing arenas. We are probably seldom as aware of our own immaturity as we are when we are nose to nose with our immature offspring.

Through it all we have to develop patience — another lesson not on the elective list. Child raising is inevitably a business of long-term rewards. In the short term, everything always seems to be changing, and nothing is ever finished. Except maybe toilet training. It sometimes does feel as if the halfway stage of that essential process goes on forever, but the bright day does come when the child trots off to the bathroom unprompted. Triumphant as that day might be, however, the satisfaction is unlikely to last for the next fifteen years or so, when you are facing different challenges that don't come to quite as clearcut a resolution.

When can you write down in the baby book that your child learned to be truthful? Which day was it that she mastered compassion towards others (including her brothers and sisters)? Was it on a Thursday or a Friday that he decided forevermore to take responsibility for his own actions, including always reporting his whereabouts to his parents, and never again wandered off with a friend or got home later than he had promised? Somewhere there may be a child who methodically scales the pinnacles of accomplishment and remains permanently perched on the peak, but my children seem to take after me, and I don't know that I've got all the lessons nailed down yet. We just barely get one area under control, and then the same challenge presents itself in a new wrapping and has to be handled all over again. We teach honesty and integrity and self-control to our toddlers, and then we teach the same principles over again in a new context when the children are racing off to grade school, and then we get to teach them even more urgently when the kids have become adolescents reaching toward adulthood. When inevitably they fail along the line, we teach them repentance — over and over and over. When is the job finished? I don't know; I haven't got that far. Not for me, and certainly not for the children.

I do know that it requires patience. Patience with the children because putting up with what they're learning not to do can drive you crazy but also patience with the job of mothering itself. Undeniably one of the satisfactions that many mothers find in the world of paid employment — whether they have to earn a paycheck or choose to — is that generally things there get done and stay done. Typing letters or teaching school or doing the buying for next fall's sportswear have elements of repetition, of course, but when a letter is finished it is mailed, and next year you will have a different class memorizing French verbs, and the only thing about the fashion industry that is predictable is that there will be novelty again the succeeding fall. Whereas at home you have the same children tripping over the same stumbling blocks, learning the same basic doctrines.

As the balance slowly tilts and more and more mothers are out in the workplace, it sometimes gets harder to accept the principle that work at home with our children is measured on a different scale. Whether a mother is home all day or has to squash her mothering into the hours that are not otherwise accounted for, she has to come to terms with the fact that her daily workload as a parent has to be counted as process and not as product. Maybe not that much changes from Monday to Tuesday. *Probably* not that much does. But bit by bit, with her absentminded remarks over her shoulder as well as with the hours spent with her full attention on the job, she is building the heritage she is passing on to the next generation. It's not anything that happens overnight, but it does happen.

And perhaps at the same time we mothers are learning one of the primary lessons we are sent to this earth to learn: that practically nothing worth having offers instant gratification. Things that can be grasped in a second usually last only that long. We arrive as babies, greedy and impatient, and, looking around at the world, there seem to be a fair number of greedy and impatient adults who still want what they want right now and don't appear ever to have learned that the treasures that have to be worked for are the ones that carry eternal value.

Our larger society presently is, after all, geared for the short term. Wanting and having are seen as properly simultaneous. Most of the advertising that fuels the media wrapped around our daily lives is designed specifically to create demands that can be satisfied right now — with a plastic credit card, if the cash isn't handy. Learning that it is the permanent pleasures that count and not the things we can grab in the ephemeral present is hard for our children to learn, and hard for us. Just as we have to teach our children that you don't run down to the store and buy candy the minute you're given your allowance, so we have to figure out that we may not get the satisfaction of immediate positive feedback from the most important things we do. It may take months, or years, or a lifetime: most of the time nobody thinks to say "thank you," and there's certainly no paycheck at the end of the week. But the love lasts forever. Maybe one of the most important blessings we gain from our mothering experience is that we are forced to slow down and appreciate what we are doing in a longer perspective.

And while our eyes are fixed on the distant horizon, how do we get from one ordinary day to the next? Well, the Lord, appreciating our restlessness even while we are trying to learn patience, did give us some milestones of child raising. Don't forget about toilet training, and the marvelous day when you dared take the spare pair of training pants out of your purse. (It's true the child probably had an accident almost immediately after that, but that doesn't count. The child was still trained.) At about the same time or maybe sooner, one otherwise ordinary Sunday also becomes a memorable milestone when your most clinging small one surprises everybody by forgetting to howl miserably when left in the nursery or the Sunbeam class, scampering off to join the teacher with never a glance back at you. Because mothers are ambivalent to the core, the relief you feel at having *that* behind you is likely to be mingled with a pang of regret that you are being outgrown. There is the day of baptism, a spiritual pause (giving thanks for the blessings so far) for an evaluation of what you've already taught and a fresh start on new responsibilities, which you can still help with but no longer assume yourself. There is the momentous twelfth birthday, when your daughter officially becomes a Young Woman, and your son, self-conscious and concentrated, joins his brother deacons and passes the sacrament. Those are the once-in-a-life-time events, prepared for and made possible by all the years of teaching the same lessons over and over again.

There is even Mother's Day. Once a year all the daily slog we do as mothers is officially appreciated. Cynics may complain that the whole event is commercialized and tacky, but I like it. I like having the occasion to concentrate on my mother, and I like having my children concentrate on me. I enjoy listening to the obligatory praise for the steadfastness and nobility of mothers. It's nice to hear it, even though I'm not much like the saintly women generally eulogized. If mothers are honored for very much the same reasons — similarly phrased — year after year, that's okay too. After all, we do very much the same things and struggle for very much the same achievements year after year. What's comforting is that at least once annually somebody notices.

It's also encouraging to discover that although the rewards are just as long-term no matter how many children you have, you get to mind less as you have more to handle. For one thing, you're busier and have less time to contemplate your life — not that you were aware of having long periods available for mulling over your life-style when you were learning how to mother on your first. It's in retrospect that life with a single child seems incomparably leisurely. But it's not just that multiple children allow less opportunity for introspection. Most of us, by the time we're coping with a second or third child, are getting more confident of our own abilities to do it and less dependent on anyone else's evaluation. It's not that we don't make mistakes: certainly if our first child doesn't teach us humility, the second and third (and subsequent) children will. It's that we discover our children survive our well-intentioned errors and love us anyway. As we adjust our expectations closer to reality, we find that even if the ultimate reward of raising a child we are proud to lead back to our Heavenly Father still shimmers in the distance, we can relax more and enjoy what's happening now. We might still leave a lot to be desired when it comes to perfection, and so may the kids, but when we take it easy and don't tie ourselves into knots about it, there are still golden moments, and hours, and even long happy days when practically everything goes right and everyone charitably overlooks the rumples that don't.

Maybe that's part of what the Eastern sages meant when they talked about the necessity for detachment, teaching that people find wisdom and happiness only when they free themselves from being driven by their desires. Maybe if we can step away from our competitive, earthbound desires — our desire to have the best-behaved children, the tidiest house, to be recognized as a woman who has her act together — then maybe we can just let the reins lie loosely in our hands and enjoy whatever this particular hour has to offer. It isn't always possible. After all, what makes the dinner hour chaos so trying is the unfortunate fact that you have to feed your family, even if in order to do it you have to step over the outraged body of your toddler who wants a book read to him *now*. Similarly, Sunday morning might be considerably more relaxed if we could all just get our families ready to go in our own good time, allowing plenty of time for dawdling and uninterrupted conversations with each other. The trouble is that sacrament meeting will, and must, start without us, and cleanliness is not the only glory of God. Punctuality also counts.

But everything isn't on a time schedule, although sometimes it feels as if it is. Whether you are home all day or just able to be with your children after work, the endless list of everything else that has to be done sometimes overwhelms the simple impulse to sit down and enjoy each other. So what if the laundry doesn't get folded? Small children, and even grown men, have been known to fish underpants out of the laundry basket instead of plucking them from neat piles in their drawers, and it never proved fatal to any of them. Dishes have sat in the sink overnight while mothers taught their children to play checkers or watched a special television show together — and it wasn't even family home evening! — and if the dishes were soaked, by next morning they are as clean as if the family activities were put on hold in the face of the greater priority of housekeeping. PTA meetings have been missed because a son needed to talk to his mother about some of the things that are confusing him, and both the national organization and the local unit survived unscathed.

There are times when we can quite legitimately put first things first.

There has been an enormous amount of nonsense talked about the relative merits of quantity and quality time—quantity time presumably being those hours when we just inhabit the same house, and quality time being when we actually pay attention to each other. Maybe what we need to consider is that we as mothers are the ones who need the quality time the most. We need those times when we can savor the sweetness of our children to sustain us through the rest of the times when the workload seems overwhelming and the end of the tunnel infinitely far.

Being a mother is a big job. It requires more un-selfishness and self-control and forbearance and pati-ence than any of us possess to start out with, and gaining as much as we need takes a lot out of us. We need to remain alertly attentive for approximately eighteen years per child, and we need the gift of discernment to distinguish genuine crises from passing flurries and the wisdom of Solomon to cope with either. Nor are all the demands emotional and spiritual. Much of moth-ering is made up of idiot tasks that have to be done every day for all the years of our parenting. We wash faces and make beds; we pick up the living room and make sure the bikes get put away under cover. We remind and we instruct and we scold and, all too briefly, we hug in passing.

Rocking a baby, walking hand-in-hand with a pre-schooler, watching your eight-year-old son chase your car up the driveway, his face alight with joy at having

you home again, an after-midnight talk with your ad-
olescent daughter struggling into her own woman-
hood — those will be the moments you will unfold and
remember once the children are grown and launched
on lives of their own. It seems only fair that we should
enjoy them and give ourselves the time to enjoy them,
while they're going on. The hours pass at the same
steady pace, however we spend them. A certain number
of them, in the inescapable nature of things, will get
used up vacuuming and dusting and doing the grocery
shopping and weeding the garden, but we must keep
some of them for us and our children. The children
need them, true enough. But we need them more.

Part of the appeal of the bobbles and cables and
textured stitches of a hand-knit sweater is that no two
bobbles are precisely alike. Neither are any two children, or, as far as that goes, any two days of a mother's
life. Each day begins with its own unique potential:
time for learning, time for teaching, time to stretch,
and time to grow. And time to focus on each other,
even if sometimes the companionship lasts only a few
seconds, like the warm sweetness of a fresh-picked
raspberry on your tongue. The years come, and the
years will go, and the elaborate pattern — the bobbles,
the cables, the intricate stitches — will be accomplished
sooner than we can believe.

But we will have the knitting of it to remember,
and we have been promised eternity.

CHAPTER 5

Eternal Patterns

Your children tug imperiously on the hem of your skirt. Your husband calls your name and expects your attention. The rest of the world seems to be queuing up to telephone you to ask you to do something — and grumbles when the line is already busy. The small still voice that reminds you that you are a daughter of God can all too easily get submerged in the hubbub of everyday noise.

Compared to the simplicity of the pattern we were knitting when we were young unattached women, the complexity of the web of patterns we find ourselves caught up in as wives and mothers sometimes seems to soak up all our available energy. There is too much to pay attention to. There are colors of frustrating subtlety (our relationships with our husbands, maybe, or the demands of running a house, perhaps the pressure of a job as well, or the continual need to scrimp financially). There are bobbles and cables and almost every other kind of flourish we can imagine (our children, whom we love and take pleasure in, who can simultaneously baffle us and exasperate us; all the other children, the ones our children play with and haggle with and who swarm all over the house; all the activities the children have to be carted around for). On bad days, it seems as if there are loose ends of yarn hanging out as far as we can see. Even on good days, it is sometimes very hard to distinguish the serene simplicity of the eternal patterns, masked as they are by all the busy elaboration of our earthly routines. But unless we are watching for them, remembering their presence, everything else we do can feel empty at the core.

It's perfectly true that keeping our minds on the eternal patterns is not necessarily easy in the midst of the distractions. Not all the distractions are worldly ones. Sometimes just trying to keep up with the practical details of fulfilling a calling at church seems to create distractions of its own. There are meetings to organize or to find time to attend. There are materials to prepare for classes we are teaching, and if we let the time get away so that the preparation is being done at the last minute, it can be hard to keep the spiritual purpose in mind in the fluster of searching magazines for suitable pictures or lettering visual aids — and getting it finished in time. Some Sundays when buttons pop off and shoes go missing and the second youngest helps herself to unsupervised handfuls of jam while you're dressing the youngest, just the mechanics of getting to church more or less on time with everyone unsticky and decked out in Sunday dress seem sufficiently daunting so that you spend the first part of the meeting breathing rapidly and calming down—which makes it difficult to get into the spirit of the meeting for the time that's left. There is no doubt that encountering the sweet innocent trust of children is a faith-promoting experience; equally, trying to corral the wiggly, easily distracted exuberance of children can be an obstacle to your own efforts to achieve a serene state of spiritual receptivity.

Even so, we do try. Although many denominations are struggling to reverse falling attendance, most of us, as active Latter-day Saint women, do get to our meetings with our families. One comforting strength the Church structure of here and now offers us is a vigorous, clearly delineated framework of activity to keep us among those present, with the safety net of home teachers and visiting teachers to help sort out problems if we fail to appear. In fact, we put in an impressive number of hours on basic church attendance. Enough so that our nonmember friends and neighbors, should they happen to discover the length of the Sunday consolidated schedule, are impressed and appalled: "*Three* hours? *With* the children?" *Going* to church usually isn't the problem.

What is more difficult is finding a way to keep your mind on what is going on, once you are there. What most of us find out during the hectic, hurried years when we are surrounded by growing children is that what should be the peaceful reverence of sacrament meeting is likely to involve much more activity than is compatible with consistent attention to the service. Children wriggle. Children fuss. They climb over their parents. They drop their binkies and their bottles, and if they can manage it, crawl under the seats into the next row looking for them. They want to wander up and down the aisles. When little, they rouse from angelic sleep to roar with surprised outrage. When older, they elbow and whisper at each other. Even a short fierce maternal glare (probably the briefest response, if not always the most effective) means you lose track of what the speaker is saying. Anything more complicated is even more distracting. It is almost impossible to maintain a spiritual line of thought while forcing a seating rearrangement among the children with one hand, the other being occupied by keeping a firm grip on the baby.

Of course ideally these problems don't arise, which means that when they do, we get further sidetracked by feeling incompetent and guilty about having obviously failed to teach the children how to behave like the children in other families who always seem to be behaving beautifully when our own are acting up. Unfortunately, just as we are trying to develop spiritual skills at our level, so are our children trying to develop at theirs, and one of the initial, and extremely difficult, lessons to learn is to behave reverently so that other people can worship undisturbed. We would not have all those lessons about reverence in Primary (or for that matter, talks about reverence in sacrament meeting) if it were a simple skill to acquire. Unavoidably a lot of the teaching has to take place on the spot, which inevitably interferes with our own worship. Few children manage to translate all the exhortation into action without diligent follow-up activity by their mothers.

Which means that you spend the meeting with only part of your attention on what you are theoretically there for. In most families, even if your husband helps, you are still the one who has to do most of the coping with the inequality between the length of sacrament meeting and the length of a child's attention span. No matter how creative your organization, no matter how hard you have worked on preparing your children, helping them learn involves remaining attentive to what is going on along the row as well as up at the pulpit. On particularly difficult Sundays, not only are we distracted from the talks we should be hearing, but Satan can tempt us with envy and covetousness when we look over the small hard heads bobbing around and bumping into us to see the older women sitting there undisturbed. Lucky souls, they can smile affectionately at our children and even retrieve the teddy bear that skidded under their feet, but they can then return their complete attention to the service, and nobody is trying to pull their earrings off their ears.

So when is there time for us to listen to the still small voice?

Maybe it would be convenient if we could suspend our own spiritual requirements for a few years while we got on with child raising. Maybe. But that's not the way it works. Everybody knows we have to nourish our bodies every day. At church we talk a lot about spiritual nourishment as being parallel, as in fact it is. What we don't talk as much about is what it feels like when we are undernourished spiritually. We know about physical hunger. Our stomachs growl and we think about food a lot. Spiritual hunger is different. It can be as insistent, but it is more ambiguous, less readily identifiable.

Spiritual malnourishment is usually what's wrong when we feel aimless and empty. The monotonous routines of family life don't seem worth the trouble. Oh, sure, we love the kids. Our marriages are okay. But in the inevitable down times, the pauses and gaps of our days, the question haunts us: "Is this all there is?" We spent our girlhoods looking forward to precisely where we are now, and now what? It's not that what you have, what you're doing, isn't good. It's fine. Great stuff, in fact. But it's not enough, and it never will be.

The voices of the world have all kinds of bright ideas about what you do about this gloomy situation. No wonder: as long as you are living in strictly worldly terms, this vague sense of malaise is likely to be a frequent companion. There are those who claim it is an inevitable result of living in a patriarchal society, and if women just could be freed to be their most independent and developed selves, the sense of something missing would disappear. Self-help authors have made their millions claiming to offer the formula for dispelling that misplaced feeling, and they suggest everything from astrology to psychological realignment to vitamins. Some of it might even help, for a while.

But the only way to cure it is to fill the emptiness. And the only way to fill the emptiness is to reestablish a spiritual connection with our Creator—and keep it open. A big meal may satisfy you after you haven't eaten all day, but that big meal today won't keep you from getting hungry tomorrow. And if there is anything as certain, it is that satisfying your spiritual hunger isn't a once-and-for-all business. It will also have to be done tomorrow, and the day after that, and the day after that. Why do you suppose we have to keep learning that, over and over again?

Just as there are breads and vegetables and dairy products that our bodies need for good nutrition, so there are different things we need spiritually. Some come easier than others. For example, one of the things we need most for our own spiritual development is to give to others. One of the main reasons that the restored Church has never gone in for institutions like contemplative monasteries or convents is that we are not meant to withdraw from the world to contemplate God and our individual relationship to him. We have been sent to this earth to be out *in* it, deeply engaged and in service to the rest of mankind here with us. We are meant to be nurturing, teaching, helping, giving ourselves and our energies away to others who need us.

Now that is something most of us have no problem arranging. As wives and mothers, as women active in the Church, we are inevitably pouring ourselves out day in, day out. We are at the service of our families twenty-four hours a day. We babysit for each other; we take around dinners when a family is having problems. Most of us serve in the schools and volunteer in our communities. If we feel spiritually desolate, it's usually not because we've been spiritually selfish. Giving occupies a lot of our daily routine.

As daughters of God, we need to share, too. We need to share publicly and privately. One of the main ways we gain from the resonance of other people's faith (and they gain from ours) is through the Church organization. We share what we have learned about the gospel in our meetings; we share the experience of working together to further the Lord's work in the administrative work we do to keep the whole enterprise functioning as it should. The priesthood may direct affairs, but everybody knows we come in for a lot of the nuts and bolts of carrying things out — and peeling peaches at a welfare cannery or decorating for a women's conference, we get a chance to share the purpose and the warmth of the gospel. Sharing is inevitably part of our busy, sociable life in the community of our ward or branch. Unless we're very isolated — which is when we appreciate how much we need that sharing — the outer circle of sharing gets taken care of in the ordinary course of life as an active Church member.

The inner circle is more personal and private. One enormous asset of a strong temple marriage is that it focuses that more intimate sharing between a man and a woman eternally joined. They can pray together, explore the scriptures together, encourage and amplify each other's spiritual progress, keep each other company through the difficult times. When that strength is not there, it's harder. But there can be sharing with your children, or your sisters in the gospel. We use family titles for each other at church—"sister," "brother"—because as members of Christ's church we are linked together as a family. Sharing the gospel as it affects your life at the most personal level was meant to take place in the home, but it happens in a good many other places as well.

As long as we're out there, involved and busy, sharing happens semiautomatically. There aren't many church callings—I can't think of any—that don't involve working closely with other people.

What doesn't get taken care of so routinely is the need each one of us feels in the deepest, most private level of our souls. As a daughter of God, each of us needs to have space and time to build and maintain a singular, private relationship with our Father in Heaven. It's that part that we sometimes miss in the rush of ordinary life, caught up in days that begin early with the sound of children's voices (or the cry of the baby just before the crack of dawn) and don't slow down until everyone else is in bed and we can collapse thankfully into sleep. It's that lack that creates the emptiness we can't quite identify.

Maybe what we need to do is rethink our spiritual priorities during these busy, child-filled years. If maintaining that singular, private relationship is the part that doesn't come easily, maybe that's what we need to concentrate on. Oh, obviously we need to keep going to church and being teachers and den mothers and

Primary and Young Women presidents and counselors or whatever, but if what we need is stillness at the center to recharge our spiritual batteries, maybe we need to figure out ways to find that as well, in spite of all the peripheral distractions that get in the way.

One suggestion that works for some women is to use some of the time when nobody else is around. If you are at home and the children nap, then naptime becomes a resource — whether for prayer, or scripture reading, or genealogy, or just peace and quiet to think about where you are in your spiritual progress and refresh your sense of our Father in Heaven's presence. If you are not at home or they don't nap — or not at the same time — then there is the possibility of extending your day a little longer or starting it a little earlier. There is an undeniable serenity about a still house in the darkness, and when the distractions are all quieted — everyone asleep and the phone finally silent — it's a marvelous freedom to move through familiar rooms so unfamiliarly empty of other people and their needs. To be able to read the scriptures and think about them, to pray wholeheartedly without being interrupted, even just to sit and read a spiritual book or magazine article with time to mull over the author's words — it becomes a way of connecting again, of filling up the empty space.

If staying up later or getting up earlier means that an already short night is further shortened, there's not a lot of point in trying it, however. Our bodies need a certain amount of sleep, and few women with small children are getting more than the minimum to start

71

with. One of the many differences between small children and adults is that adults routinely sleep all night long or at least don't insist on waking other people up if they do rouse. Small children like company when they wake up and it's dark. Or they jerk awake with nightmares or teething, and they need you. For years mothers live with the reality of broken sleep. In the laboratory they call it experimentation with sleep deprivation and the subjects, at the end of the experiment, are sent home for a good healthy rest. When it happens at home, it's called real life, and it is assumed you will rise ready for the day whether or not you've been up and down all night and the night before that.

When you are going full speed from the time you wake until you fall into bed, you get tired. You get *really* tired, and deciding to ignore it doesn't help. Fatigue has certain physical consequences. One is that mental processes slow down, so that you wind up reading the same scripture verses over and over or get stuck in the middle of a prayer and find yourself repeating the same routine phrases instead of really thinking about what you're saying. Stubbornly persevering in staying up late or getting up early because you feel you can somehow find some extra time there misses the whole point of what you're trying to do. If you're too tired to think (and if you're wondering about it, you probably are), you might just as well go to bed. You'll have to find some other time for your spiritual program, but you can comfort yourself with the recognition that going to sleep at the same time as your husband — or getting up with him—has advantages of its own. After all, that's a relationship that needs maintenance too.

What you need, in fact, is whatever works. If cutting back on your sleep isn't a reasonable alternative, maybe you can sit the kids in front of a suitable tape or television program for an hour or so and retreat to the next room. You wouldn't want to do it all day, but an hour isn't going to hurt them and may well make the difference for you. Maybe you'll find a different time every day. Maybe, some days, there won't be a chunk of time at all, but only a few snatched moments kneeling behind a closed bathroom door because you thought it might be marginally less likely that the children would follow you there. Never mind: be assured that the Lord hears prayers from there just as he hears them from anywhere else.

When trying to work out how to fit personal spirituality into our lives, we have to remember that no solution will be a permanent one. Circumstances change, and so must our responses to them. What works for one stage of family life needs reshuffling for another. When we are feeling most buffeted and surrounded by everything that has to be done, it helps to remember that this time in our lives won't last forever. It was not always this way (remember before you were married, when not only could you pay attention in sacrament meeting but could spend almost unlimited time before church deciding what to wear and applying your makeup?) and it won't always be. Remember those good sisters, unencumbered by squirming children, sitting next to their husbands in the easy comfort of long habit? That will be you. What we have is a temporary problem. For the time being, we are trying to meet eternal necessities with a temporary Band-Aid, of whatever dimensions are required.

The methods of filling spiritual needs are the obvious ones that we've been counseled about for years. We just have to put them into practice. The incomparable peace of the temple is always available. It is easier if there is one within convenient range, but even if there isn't yet, the rewards of temple attendance are worth whatever effort it takes to get there — probably true most of all for us, who are in such need of peace. It's an unfortunate temptation to allow ourselves to be daunted by logistical difficulties. Do we too often leave the responsibility for temple work to the older women who don't have to find someone to look after their children, not realizing that the tranquility of a place utterly removed from the press and flow of our everyday lives is precisely what we are hungry for? Within those sacred walls we are not primarily either wives or mothers — we are the daughters of our Father in Heaven, and for a few hours we can come home.

Another spiritual tool adapted to our needs during these busy years is the power of fasting and prayer. Fasting and prayer is not something worked out just for these latter days — it has been a part of religious observance down the centuries in virtually all cultures and all circumstances. The major religions of the world have all used fasting and prayer as a method to concentrate a worshipper's focus. It has always been used because it always works.

For us, one of its great strengths is its flexibility. You don't have to be anywhere special to fast. You don't need anybody else to participate. You can fast in your own home, while you take care of the children and fold the laundry or vacuum the floor, or at work, while you get on with your assigned duties. It can be an intensely private way of building a relationship with the Lord, or it can be a way to teach your children by your example that your spiritual life is important enough to you to devote your day to it.

Fasting can be used for lots of purposes. For us as a people, the most common is obviously the regular monthly fast. Apart from Fast Sunday, most of us tend to use fasting primarily as a method of obtaining special closeness to the Lord, because we are in need of some particular blessing, or because we need guidance in making a difficult or important decision. Or there are the times when we join as a family—or as a ward family—to fast together to plead for a blessing for one individual who is in need. We are used to thinking of fasting when we think about those needs.

We might not think of fasting as a way to work through an undefined feeling of pointlessness, although that is exactly when the spiritual power might help us most. Or when we are so harrassed by the sense of being tugged in a thousand different directions (now it's finding where the baby left her blanket so she'll settle down for her nap; now it's trying to figure out what's jammed the garbage disposal) that we can't focus on an eternal dimension. At least not here, not now. Or when we are feeling specifically disconnected from the Spirit. But one of the best ways to focus, to reconnect, is to use the tool of the fast.

We fast because the Lord has told us to do so, but there are some practical reasons why it works. For one, fasting reorders our daily routines and thus holds our attention. Eating plays an enormous role in our lives. Choosing not to eat reminds us continually that there is something else going on today. Every time you move automatically toward the kitchen but stop, your thoughts inevitably turn to what you are fasting about. When your stomach burbles, you remember. Whenever the thought of food crosses your consciousness, you remember. You can be doing all the things you would be doing on any other ordinary day, and yet your thoughts are brought back over and over to your fast and the reasons for it.

Which is one reason fasting is such a source of spiritual strength — if we take advantage of all the continual reminders our bodies give us, and use them as reminders to pray. Without prayer, fasting is simply missing a couple of meals. People skip meals all the time, and it doesn't do a thing for their spiritual lives, because spirituality had no part in it. One of the most important elements of fasting is the deliberate decision to discipline the ordinary desires of the body and give precedence to the soul — and that precedence comes out in our prayers. We can pray silently while rocking the baby or while sitting in front of a computer or in the temporary privacy of a bedroom or the front seat of the car. We can pray out loud in the quiet of any room available to us.

Sometimes when I am fasting I feel as if my thoughts become a stream-of-consciousness kind of prayer—a rippling commentary on my day and the concerns that have brought me to fast. For the period of my fast, my ordinary life becomes an intrusion on my dialogue with the Lord, instead of the other way around. The people I deal with probably dismiss my abstraction as absent-mindedness, and goodness knows I am often enough absentminded for less worthy reasons. Although I may never step out of the door, it is as if I have been away for the day. It wouldn't be fair to the family to do it every day, nor is that required of us. Most days we are wholly available to those who depend on us. But we are refreshed by the days when we are most available to the Lord.

For me, one auxiliary benefit of fasting is that it reminds me that being hungry is uncomfortable and encourages me to think about all the people—God's sons and daughters, as much as I am—for whom going without is not a matter of choice. Naturally, Fast Sunday and fast offerings are a regular reminder, but I think it's good for me to be reminded in between times. I need to keep remembering that it is an incomparable blessing to have food in the kitchen cupboards for my children.

It is a good blessing to be reminded of when I have had a week of having them surging noisily around me—maybe a winter week of school vacation—and I've been stuck in the frame of mind to be exasperated by all the annoying things they do and the even longer list of things they forget to do. Pricked by my own hunger (which I know I will satisfy as soon as I end my fast), I can imagine what it would be like if they were hungry and I had no food. In that moment of desperation — even imagined desperation — I recognize how much I would suffer and am surprised all over again by the revelation of how dearly I love them. Counting blessings is only one of the spiritual exercises fasting and prayer precipitates, but it's a useful exercise for the days when it's easy to forget how blessed we are just to have a family, whether or not they are behaving precisely as we'd like.

Another method of filling our spiritual need is the patient work of genealogy. Too often we are tempted to leave that to our older relatives, who seem to have the time available to follow out lines of research and sift through piles of old documents and letters. But we, too, can use the peace and spiritual strength that comes from active connection with our forebears and the satisfying exultation of making sure that their ordinances are completed as they should be. Not least, genealogy involves using our brains in a way that most of the rest of our work in looking after the physical well-being of a family does not. It feels good to have to think, to puzzle out connections and make the leaps of guesswork in tracing an ancestor, and then to see if you can locate the documentation to prove you guessed right. Of course there's more risk of misplacing something in a home where there are small hands that carry things away than in an all-adult household, but what on earth was the shoe box invented for if not to be a convenient container (with a lid!) to keep genealogical papers out of tempting range. Filing cabinets are fine — if you have the space and the finances — but a row of shoe boxes can work just as well, and since you're likely to have short stretches of time rather than long hours in which to work, a shoe box is handy and portable and can easily accommodate what you're working on right then.

What you do in the way of a personal spiritual activity is less important than *that* you do. It's a sad commentary on the state of my spiritual development that too often it takes not being able to do something to make me appreciate it. All the years when there were hours upon hours that I might have dedicated to expanding my spirituality, generally I chose not to. Or at least not nearly as often as I could have. Now, when the minutes have to be carved out of something else, they are particularly precious, and not only do I benefit from them but I savor the benefiting.

If I were a little closer to perfection, that recognition would probably be so comforting that I would stop fussing about the times when circumstances get in the way of participating fully in an ordinary, predictable form of worship — sacrament meeting, for example. As perfection is still a good way off, it is sometimes hard to appreciate that an exasperating distraction can be thought of as a blessing. Especially when I am sitting there in the meeting trying to listen to a talk that sounds interesting, and my son is whispering that he needs to go to the bathroom (second time so far, and there is another speaker to go). I am consequently torn between trying to follow the speaker's line of thought and trying to decide if we have a physical problem here or excessive restlessness. At such moments, reminding myself that these frustrations during meetings make my hasty moments of prayer or scripture reading at home more rewarding seems too dismally Pollyannaish for words. But whether or not I choose to count the blessing right then, a blessing it is.

Of course, in some ways I pamper myself in the ways I meet my spiritual needs. When there doesn't seem to be any peaceful time available for scripture reading, for example, I find it works best if I don't confine myself to a program of reading that to be done properly requires blocks of time. For me, setting out to study a particular passage or work my way through one book methodically needs a period of uninterrupted concentration. When I know there's every chance I'm going to have to stop in the middle for one reason or another, I do better to open to passages I know well and love—for me, the Psalms, or Isaiah, or maybe the life of Jesus in one of the Gospels or 3 Nephi, or maybe one of Paul's epistles—and then even if I'm right and the phone rings or somebody bobs up to call me back to duty, the words I know will sing on in the back of my mind while I cope with whatever domestic emergency suddenly required attention.

Other words could be singing in my head while my hands are busy. My grandmother sang hymns while she did her ordinary jobs around the house, and it is one of the things about her that my mother remembers with nostalgia and affection. I would love to have my children remember that about me, but first I have to turn off the radio or television or other noisy distraction from my end of the century, and second I have to learn enough hymns so that my repertoire is not limited to "Come, Come Ye Saints" and maybe a verse or two from a couple of others. If I propped the hymnbook up behind the kitchen faucets, I could memorize words while peeling potatoes or rinsing dishes for the dishwasher, and the inevitable water spots on the pages could be dedicated to the greater glory of God, as my Catholic friends so engagingly phrase it. It would have been nice if the Lord had blessed me with a more beautiful voice with which to carol his praises, but in my experience the children (who are likely to be my only audience) were remarkably uncritical about their lullabies. If their standards have risen since, that would just be too bad. Since in the first place the exercise would be for *me*, what I sound like would be distinctly secondary.

In any case, it would serve as a reminder to me that all communion with our Heavenly Father does not have to be conducted in a funeral hush. Although there are unquestionably times when I long for peace and stillness to soothe my soul, I have to recognize that we were sent here to live in the noisy world, to be a part of it, and to learn how to remain close to the Lord in spite of it all. It is as if the Lord has made his eternal patterns deliberately subtle, so that we have to peer through all the fussy elaboration of our earthly knitting to remember the ways they go.

Even my beloved Psalms, those songs of praise, are songs written by men fully engaged in the business of living. They make constant references to the practical objects of everyday living. David and the other psalmists sang of the glory of God, true enough, but they also sang about babes and bows and arrows and beds and cups and pots and sheep and oxen and fish. Their worship of God took place in a concrete real world, full of real people who were wicked, and sinners who repent, and the righteous who were getting the short end of the stick and counted on their Father in Heaven and his goodness to help them survive their trials. Not for them the artificial peace of a haven protected from the glories and agonies — and ordinary frustrations — of everyday living. Life was good, or life was hard, but either way they acknowledged the presence and the might of their God.

As we must do. Without acknowledging God, our life would be nothing but pointless routine, all our dedication to our children of no particular benefit except to train them to undertake, eventually, exactly the same pointless routine. With it, even the most maddening frustrations are a step on the ladder on our way home to our Father, and our most critical job is to teach our children to look homeward with us. We are told over and over again that what happens to us isn't important. It's what we do about it, how we respond, that matters. Our lives are difficult, sometimes. They're meant to be. We would learn very little from our experience in mortality if all we faced was a golden glide back into eternity.

Sometimes, encouraged by all the propaganda about how hard done by women are in a society structured (they say) for and by men, we get to feeling that we, as women, have a particularly difficult time. That hemmed in by our responsibilities as wives and mothers it's more difficult for us to have a clear shot at establishing a clear relationship with our Father in Heaven. Men have it better, we might grumble. They have the priesthood. They have the leadership.

Which is true, and which means they have their own set of obstacles. We're not unique. If we find that the practical details of coping with babies and children and family relationships get in the way of our spirituality, they find that the practical details of organizing God's church in the here and now (depending on fallible human beings, who fall through on commitments and repent and sometimes fall through again) may keep their minds more attentive to the structure than to the meaning behind it. All of us, men and women alike, battle distraction from the meaningful, a distraction that renders the rest of life meaningless.

All of us, fundamentally, have to develop the same skills, even though we may come to them by different paths. Our job on this earth is to learn to sort out the message of the gospel, to hear our Father's voice through the hubbub of everyone else's. We have to learn to discern and treasure the *real* pattern, the eternal pattern, through all the elaboration of the foreground, which is intrinsically a part of our life on this earth, and will pass, as we have been promised, "in the twinkling of an eye."

Each of us has to figure out our own way to master those skills, and the creativity we put into it is what makes living on this earth such an interesting exercise, so full of variety and individuality. We each have the job of framing our personal preferences into the eternal patterns. We spend our money differently, for example. I love pictures on my wall and books on my shelves, and sit reasonably contentedly on shabby furniture while admiring them; my sister at church may prefer sleek upholstery and deep carpets instead, but both of us know we must pay the Lord's tenth before we make our decisions on how to spend the nine-tenths left over. We may have entirely different kinds of marriages — her husband blond and bouncy and outgoing, with an active social life important to them both, my husband darker and more reserved, with a preference like mine for quiet evenings at home — but we are alike in the importance we both give to fidelity and the strength of family bonds. We both obey the Word of Wisdom, but she serves icy mineral water in her crystal glasses, and I serve bubbly grape juice in mine.

In following the pattern of our everyday spiritual lives there is room for creativity — but the patterns themselves, as we uncover them, are eternal and unchanging. Our relationship with our Father in Heaven, even on the busiest, most hectic, exasperating days, endures, solid and sure under the flotsam of transient mortality. The emptiness of the bad days, the sense of misplacement, is nothing more in reality than an illusion. As his daughters, if we reach out to him, surrounded by confusion though we might be, we will always find him. He was with us before, and if we can just hang on, he will be with us still. He is, after all, always there. It is only we who are sometimes found missing in action.

CHAPTER 6

The Secret Needles

I like to walk in the early morning. I walk partly for the physical exercise, to rev up my metabolism and burn off some excess calories before I think about breakfast. But that's only part of it. Part of it is so that I will have forty minutes or so all to myself. There's no phone, and everyone else is sleeping back at home. Sometimes I take along a tape player and headphones, but more often I just walk, listening to the sounds I hear as I pass, comfortable with the silence. I seem to live a very noisy life, full of voices and doors banging and music and the television chattering—and I obviously choose to do so, because as often as not I am the one who automatically reaches out for the knob to turn on a radio or TV when I come into an empty room. But the silence of the early morning seeps into my consciousness and refreshes me.

I live near what we now call a little lake. It used to be the millpond, back in the days when my town was a self-sufficient community and not the bedroom suburb it has become. Beyond the waterfall is a white house with green shutters that used to be a cider mill. Somebody lives there now, and I often wonder how you would adapt the floorplan of a cider mill (even a nineteenth-century cider mill) to the requirements of modern domestic living. It's very satisfying, somehow, to have time to wonder about things like that, or to measure my footsteps so that they fall between the cement lines of the sidewalks. One step in one square, two in the next: don't step on a crack, you'll break your mother's back. Funny to consider that when my children chant that, it's my back they're talking about. Out here alone, even on familiar streets, the reality of my life as somebody's mother, somebody else's wife, seems to waver and fade. Walking along, wrapped in my silence, I am singularly *me*.

Other people don't seem to see that when they look at me. What they see is a grown woman with busy knitting needles clacking, spewing out row after row of a wife's pattern, a mother's pattern, making the phone calls, assembling the armloads of stuff to be carted up to the church and back home again, doing the grocery shopping, packing children into the car, cooking the dinners and making the beds. They don't see the silent secret needles that are working away simultaneously in private somewhere on the fabric that is my own self. Sometimes it's even hard for me to see it. Walking through a store, I catch sight of my reflection in a mirror and there's a preoccupied woman glancing back at me, eerily reminiscent of my mother but oddly dressed in the sweater and skirt I put on this morning. Is that me? What happened to the girl I remember being me? Where did she go?

For it's absolutely certain she's not here now. That girl was young and unsure and very inexperienced: she didn't know any of the things that make up the fabric of my life now. She didn't know how to make a dinner without using recipes; she didn't know how to tell by the tightening of her husband's lips when he has had enough; she couldn't judge by the sound of the cry whether the fallen child was hurt or just indignant. She didn't know that boiling water miraculously erases fruit stains, and she didn't know, except maybe in theory, how to get a kitchen thoroughly clean, or that you need to do it so often. She didn't know what it's like to really love a man, even when you are weary and exasperated with him. She didn't know the panicky fluttering you feel when you sit with your injured child in your arms while the hospital emergency triage nurse writes up his papers. She had never taken a beloved family pet to the veterinarian to be put to sleep; she had never seen the magical joy on her toddler's face when she saw the lights come up on her first Christmas tree.

Of course in some ways we are alike. We look more or less similar, if you overlook a few extra pounds on me now, a little more looseness of the skin, and the first spurts of gray hair. I know how to dress to suit my looks better than she did, but she was working and unmarried and could afford to purchase clothes more enthusiastically than I can. Many of our interests are the same: she loved to read, as I do; she had just discovered the music that delights and comforts me; we both knit. We like a lot of the same people. But she was less selective about movies than I have come to be, and she had never experimented with the peaceful pleasures of cross-stitch. We are alike in our spasms of restlessness — only she was restless with her impatience to get her life started, wondering what it would be like, and I am sometimes restless with the sense that my life is sweeping me along so rapidly that I am losing touch with whoever the me who exists now really is.

But why would that matter?

Because that essential me is a composite of all the other roles I carry, and if I am to be able to continue to meet the needs of everyone else, I must somehow determine my own. Which is not to say that my needs necessarily take priority. There are clearly times when they do not. But unless I can work out what my needs are, there's no rational way to work out what the priorities should be.

And what are those needs? Well, when I think about them I don't believe they are so different from anyone else's. I suppose, trying to categorize them as broadly as possible, that I — that *we* — need three things. The first is very simple: we need to feel that we are loved. Just plain old unvarnished unconditional love. Second, we need to have some sort of structure or discipline in our lives. We need to feel that there is some rational sense to the way we spend our days. And third, we need to feel that we have some independent worth:

that what we are is more than being somebody's wife, somebody else's mother. I need to be valued for whatever it is I am.

We all know love is a basic need, but we get so used to thinking about how we should give it out that it seems sort of self-indulgent to consider how we get it. Still, we need to feel loved just as much as those scraggly leggy growing kids of ours do, leaning momentarily against us before they dash off again on one of their mysterious projects. We need to have the warm security of knowing love is there; we need to know that if we reach out a hand, someone will take it. Sometimes we need to lean, too.

When we get into trouble is when we expect that those around us will be able to meet those needs of ours consistently, in the same way every time. And they can't and won't. Love doesn't work like that. Love ebbs and flows, but it goes on being love. We are used to the fluctuations in our own feelings. I know, for example, that I don't love my husband exactly the same way every day. We go through periods of living more like roommates, bumping up against each other matter-of-factly in the ordinary course of living in the same house. I'm busy; he's busy. Love ebbs. Then something happens: *I* don't know what it is. Maybe I get a little extra sleep one night, maybe he does — maybe something nice comes in the mail. Maybe he says something that makes me laugh and look at him, really look at him, for the first time in days. Maybe absolutely nothing I can identify happens. But one day we decide on the spur of the moment to go out for ice cream together after dinner, or maybe I suddenly feel like giving him a hug, and it isn't just roommates any more. Love flows back up around us again, warm and familiar.

Now none of that worries me when I'm the one who withdrew for a while, or if it's a mutual if unacknowledged cool spell. If, in the middle of it, people asked me if I loved my husband, I'd look at them as if they'd lost their minds. Of course I love him, I'd say impatiently. Who's talking about love here? I'm just busy. So's he. What's the problem?

So why does it sometimes worry me when it's the other way around, when I sense that he is not quite there with me? Maybe he patted my hand absentmindedly when I expected him to grasp it. Maybe he's staring off into space when I thought I would turn to meet his eyes. I feel cold. I brood. It's gone for good, I decide gloomily. This is the way our marriage will now be. It didn't used to be like this. It wasn't like this in the beginning.

And of course in the beginning it wasn't, because love then was too simple and shallow. It was beginner's love, like a beginner's piano piece played with one hand on five keys. It's when love stretches out and grows to encompass all the keys on the piano, to require both hands and incorporate all the fluctuations of an adult relationship that you begin to feel the rhythm and constancy behind the variations. "When you love someone you do not love them all the time, in exactly the same way, from moment to moment," Anne Morrow Lindbergh wrote in *Gift from the Sea.* "And yet this is exactly what most of us demand. . . . We insist on permanency, on duration, on continuity; when the only continuity possible, in life as in love, is in growth, in fluidity—in freedom, in the sense that the dancers are free, barely touching as they pass, but partners in the same pattern."

Maybe what we need to learn is trust. Trust in each other, and trust in love itself. We don't assume that our teenage children don't love us when they don't talk much to us for a week at a time. If everything else seems to be proceeding routinely, we shrug and say it's just a stage—and sure enough, a day or two later they flop down in the kitchen and we find ourselves chatting as if nothing had ever happened, as in a sense nothing did. Maybe what we need to remember is that we can't live life on a high note permanently: peaks need to be set off by more prosaic plains and valleys on either side. What counts is the shape of our love as a whole. It's true that marriages do stale and adolescents do become estranged, but usually there are a lot more symptoms than simply a cool spell that lasts a few days. (If you're genuinely worried, maybe you should be the one to suggest dinner out—if the budget can possibly stand it—for just the two of you, or figure out some opportunity to get an uninterrupted unpressured half hour with your teenager and check what the temperature of the relationship really is.)

Most of us just need to learn to trust the cycles in love—the ups and downs in other people's feelings, as in our own. You can't catch the high tide on the beach and hold it there, but the ocean hasn't ceased to exist as it slips back down the sand away from your fingers.

As it slipped away, so it will rush back up to you. We do need love, but we also need to learn to recognize love in all its phases—not to clutch at what can't be held and not to underestimate the constancy of the people around us.

Sometimes all that is needed is to allow space for us to be loved. We are so busy—too busy, often, for those who love us to catch us to tell us so. If you sometimes feel you've lost track of the girl you used to be, just think what it must be like for your husband. He fell in love and married that girl, and now sometimes all he can find is the speeding blur through the kitchen or out the back door. He now has a wife who is perpetually surrounded by other responsibilities and concerns. How can he give her a spontaneous hug if she always has a child in her arms or is struggling into a coat, car keys in hand, or responds to his greeting with an absentminded "Ummm?" over her shoulder as she peers anxiously into the oven. In a perfect world he would know exactly what to say to stop her dead in her tracks long enough for him to let her know he still loves her. In the real world, a lot of husbands retreat, perplexed.

Maybe what we need to do is stop the merry-go-round long enough to give those people we love a chance. We need to allow space and time to be loved. We need to spend time alone—alone with our husbands, alone with each of our children. Maybe not every day: there are realistic limits to what twenty-four hours can accommodate. But often enough. We need lazy, unprogrammed time: dawdling over dinner for two, perhaps, or taking a walk together, or just sitting out in the car for a few minutes instead of bolting out the second the ignition is flicked off and back into the house to accomplish the next seventeen items on the list. We need to pay attention long enough to hear what they have to tell us. Because, after all, we love them too.

The whole problem wouldn't come up, of course, if we were not so genuinely busy. Usually it's not that we're hiding from our husbands or our children behind a facade of makework jobs. We just plain have more to do than is reasonably accomplishable. Which means that almost every day there are things on today's list left over that have to get tacked on to tomorrow's, which means tomorrow gets even busier, and so on. The people who make it their business to calculate these sorts of things report that we now have ten less hours of leisure time per week than people had twenty years ago, and whether or not we have statistical support for that individually, it feels true.

We live in the age of feminist excellence, when as a woman you are supposed to be competent in everything. You can tend babies, run a household, seduce your husband, earn your own living if necessary, match intelligence with anyone, be as knowledgeable about problems halfway around the world as you are about the ones in your own community, understand adolescents and tax forms, keep your body lithe and well-exercised, function with the skill and enthusiasm of a master gardener, know which movies or rock albums are off-limits for your kids and why, and oh, yes, cook divinely and economically. There are a few cautionary voices murmuring deprecatingly that you might not be able to do all of it at the same time. Oh, great. The difficulty comes in knowing which standards to scuttle. They're all important, and you want to get it right. In a world in which success is glorified, how do you resign yourself to selective incompetence?

I know perfectly well that every generation believes itself frustrated by wholly unique difficulties, but even so, it seems to me that we have at present a situation in which the acceptable minimum for a woman's performance is at an unprecedented high. What we expect of ourselves is mind-boggling. For one thing, taking the population as a whole, most American women are now part of the work force, part time or full time. When the average woman takes on a paying job, what she becomes responsible for is two jobs: the one for which she gets her paycheck, and the other one, which is doing practically everything she (or her mother) used to do at home as well. If she is very fortunate and her husband, if she has one, does half the work at home (which, statistically speaking, means she falls into about 10 percent of the population), she only has to cope with one and a half jobs. Lucky woman.

If, on the other hand, she is able to choose to stay home, then clearly to be a success she must do a slap-up, super-duper job, providing Quality Time every hour of the day and do it on the kind of budget you have to live on with a single income these days. Get tired just chasing the toddler all day, half the time carrying the baby? Gee, you can nap any time you want. Think of those poor mothers who drag home from the office

94

to face their lively offspring. You mean your house doesn't look fit for company all the time, whether or not the kids have their friends over? You mean your furniture's getting a little worn, and you aren't taking upholstery classes to learn how to rejuvenate it? You mean you didn't leap at the opportunity to substitute in Primary last Sunday? You mean you don't bake your own bread? You mean you didn't get all the laundry finished yet and it's dinnertime? What *do* you do all day?

Among the more interesting themes of recent feminist writing is a consideration of housework. Ann Oakley, a British woman who was among the first to take it seriously, wrote that her decision to do a postgraduate study of women's attitudes toward housework as work was met with patronizing hilarity by her male professors. Since then, the idea that housework is in fact genuine work and therefore as significant as any other form of labor has made a bit more headway. One recent study presented the startling(!) idea that women in fact do *more* housework than they used to do in the days before laborsaving machinery, mainly because most of the laborsaving machinery saves labor that either men or the children or servants previously did. (Up until the early years of this century, remember, you didn't have to be rich to have a hired girl to help out.) Also, our standards are considerably higher. Not many of us have a wardrobe consisting in total of a work dress for everyday and a Sunday dress for best. Nor do our children. Can you imagine the expression on the face of your daughter if you proposed that two outfits were all she needed to have in this world? No way did those work clothes get washed after every wearing. Now not only our clothes but our houses are kept much cleaner, and they are filled with vastly greater numbers of possessions that need maintenance. Would anyone have tried to set off across the plains with one-tenth of what we consider essential for normal living?

But of course it isn't just the housework. We expect ourselves to do everything we read about in the magazines or hear about in Relief Society and do it well or be learning to do it well. We expect ourselves to be obedient followers, gentle leaders, inspiring teachers, compassionate sisters, and well-informed scriptorians. We expect to be involved in all the extras: Primary parties, Young Women/Young Men activities, Relief Society socials, quorum gatherings — somebody has to figure out what's going on, organize the food, get it there, keep things going, and clean up afterwards, and usually the somebody is us.

There is all the time in the car. Quite apart from driving back and forth from church (which, if you don't live in the heart of Zion, may involve a considerable journey), there are the routine trips, like grocery shopping and taking your son down to the mall for another pair of shoes he can outgrow in six weeks flat. Your children have lessons and sports they need to be driven to and friends they want to see who live just beyond bike range. There are the endless errands. There are school activities: escorting kids on excursions, participating in fund-raisers, dropping off the lunch or the gym clothes that were forgotten at home.

There are all the organizations that need volunteers. Everywhere there are the essential and the semiessential community activities, which, with the rising numbers of women in the work force, need volunteers more desperately than ever before. As Latter-day Saint women, we are urged to take part in community affairs. We can hardly sit around and complain about community standards if we hang back from getting involved. But it means more meetings to attend, and more preparation time at home and more time on the telephone.

The point isn't that none of us do all of it. The point is that most of us have the nagging feeling that we should be doing more of it than we are managing so far. It's not a particularly comfortable sensation. Just as we need to feel we are loved, we need to feel that we're doing a reasonable job of whatever makes up the routine of our daily lives. Love in good working order may be the background of our individual lives, but if the foreground is a haphazard mess of dropped stitches and loose threads, there's not much satisfaction in claiming the whole thing as a finished product. We need some discipline and structure to help us see the shape in what we're doing, some way of determining our personal priorities so that at the end of most days we feel the important things did get done, and it's only the extra stuff that will have to get finished tomorrow (we hope).

The plain fact is that none of us can do everything people ask us to do or that we might wish we could do. You can't do everything if you're trying to meet family responsibilities and hold down an outside job, and you still can't do everything even if you're home all day. There are always more people with ideas about what you could do in what might loosely be called your spare time than there is spare time in existence. Looked at from their point of view, the project each of them is pushing is the most important project around. So they bubble with enthusiasm and point out just how vital whateveritis is and how much you are needed (or, alternatively, how much you will enjoy doing it).

What you have to remember is that you can't say yes to all of them. If you're too busy to start with, you can't even follow through on every bright idea you have yourself, unless you're prepared to make time by giving up something else already on your agenda. It is an insidious temptation to believe that taking on extra activities will spur you into greater efficiency. Maybe, if you are in the delicious position of having some slack time on your hands, that might be true—to a point. Pressure does force us to greater feats of organization. All those cliches about "if you want something done, ask a busy person to do it" came from somewhere. But unless you are one of those superenergized women who make the rest of us marvel, you're not going to be able to keep it up indefinitely. And even if you can, the people around you—the ones you love—may not be able to keep up with you.

The trouble for me is that in the family context, efficiency (in the sense of getting as much packed into the day as possible) comes at a price. I find that my husband and I, and the children and I, and even, I think, the Lord and I need to have a bit of give in the schedule. It's all very well for me to have blocked out half an hour to spend with my fifteen-year-old, for example, but usually it works out that she is unavailable then—either because she's doing something else or because she happens to be feeling uncommunicative. When she needs that half hour may be an hour later, or a week later, or at twelve some night. (She is, after all, fifteen, and adolescents seem to be nocturnal animals.) When I've packed my day like a sausage skin, the later time slot may not be available, and by midnight of a day when I never stopped I'm too sleepy for sensible conversation.

The same kind of thing happens with my husband, although not being fifteen, he's nicer about it. Still, when he wants to talk to me about something, he would prefer to talk about it then; and if I insist it has to be postponed until later, if it's nothing of major importance, his enthusiasm is likely to have waned, and instead of a full discussion when I've got time for it, I get the shorthand version.

To a certain extent it happens with the Lord too, only then the problem is on my side. I find it hard to slide into a devotional mood just like that, because now is when the schedule says I should—and then move on to something else in precisely fifteen minutes. I need to have my schedule fit me and not the other way around. I need to know I can stop and take the time to do something totally spontaneous—whether it might be a breezy chat, or heart-to-heart revelations, a prayer of supplication or thanksgiving, or even time just to sit with my legs stretched out enjoying the first warm spring afternoon with a daughter — without having my whole day collapse around me like a house of cards. Time management experts may insist that with proper organization there is a way to get it all done, but rigid time management skills don't seem perfectly suited for the intricate cat's cradle of a family.

The obvious necessity is to make up a list of priorities. When I do that, I generally begin by putting down my relationship with Heavenly Father first, then my husband, then my children, and then everything else. Which are undoubtedly the priorities I want to have, but when it comes to applying them on any given Wednesday, the list is not very enlightening, because there are always times when primary urgencies of a lesser priority take precedence over secondary urgencies of a greater priority. Or, in other words, sometimes I have to take my son for his piano lesson even if it means I won't get to the cleaner to pick up my husband's suit. In the long run, my husband is the more important, but he isn't going to wear that suit tomorrow anyway, and if my son is ever going to learn how to play the piano, he has to show up for his lesson. To make a priority list that is going to do me any good, I have to get down to that kind of detail. Sometimes I get the priorities wrong, but that's why I give thanks for the delicious luxury of having another day that will begin tomorrow in which I can rearrange things.

Most of all, for my own sake, I need to feel that my days are adding up to something. The days when I feel most out of touch with myself are the days when I am rushing from one job to the next, handing out bite-size pieces of myself to everybody, which never add up to anything. I need to give, yes. And not all of it will add up to a meaningful contribution. But most of it should. I need to make that conscious list of my priorities for *this* time of my life, because inevitably my life will change, and so too will the priorities. But then I have to recognize that some of the items that fall further down the list may be valid, may be important, but still may have to be laid aside while a higher priority is in hand. Everything cannot be first priority, or nothing is.

I need to have my days add up to something because I need to feel that I add up to something. Me. Not Mrs. Somebody, or somebody's mother, but me.

It's not always the easiest feeling to maintain. We're hard on ourselves. We get so used to contemplating our faults that we forget to give ourselves credit for our virtues. Other people get so used to taking our contributions for granted that they simply don't think to mention them. Or they're too young and unobservant. When is the last time anyone expressed admiration for the way you get the laundry done, week after week, or for the polish on the kitchen floor? Or (if housekeeping talents are not what you would most like to be appreciated for) for keeping your own temper while coping with the tantrum of a balky two-year-old or thirteen-year-old? How about some recognition for the number of parent-teacher conferences you have faithfully attended? Or for making sure that the household pets get fed whether or not anyone else remembers? It would be nice just to have someone notice how many times you manage to back the car out of the garage without driving over the bikes parked haphazardly along the sides — in my experience what the family remembers is the time you did back over one and the sixteen dollars it cost for a new wheel.

I wouldn't be surprised if money didn't have quite a bit to do with the distinction between achievements people notice and achievements they don't. We live in a very materialistic society, in which most things are evaluated by what they are worth in a monetary sense. The majority of what we do as wives and mothers simply can't be assessed that way. There's no way to attach a price tag to toilet training or restoring a husband's sense of himself when a project he had spent months on came to nothing. Nor is there a way to figure out what it would cost to get someone to spend twenty-four hours a day raising, say, five children to reasonably well-balanced maturity, over a thirty-year period. You can't hire someone to take on that kind of job, but mothers do it all the time.

It's bad enough when other people dismiss what we do at home as less prestigious because we don't get paid for it. It's infinitely worse if we humbly agree with them. Everything in life doesn't have to have a price attached, and if we allow ourselves to feel devalued, we are buying into the idea that the monetary standard is the important one. We know that's not true. We need to insist that there are other valid measures besides dollars and cents, not only for our own sakes, but for our daughters'. But we may have to tell ourselves that the loudest.

It is particularly encouraging, sometimes, to be told

that some things we do quite routinely and totally non-commercially might be considered valuable. The anthropologist Mary Catherine Bateson points out that as women we develop certain skills that are beneficial to our entire society, particularly as women come to play a more active role in public life. "You know what people say about women," she has said. "That they're easily distracted, and that success has to do with focusing on specific goals. But what if the health of the world depends on the same kind of capacity that allows you, while you're feeding one child, to see that the other child is reaching up and about to pull a cooking pot of hot liquid on his head? This capacity to see out of the corner of your eye, and care about the health, not just of one child, but of three or four and a husband and other members of the family — this is the beginning of the capacity to care about the health of a multitude of nations, or an environment of many species."

From the first day I brought the first baby home and settled down to live there with one baby, one husband, and me, I had to learn those skills. I had two people with two different kinds of needs, and they had to be interlaced together. As the other children came along, my skills had to multiply. I had to be able to wipe a nose, help with arithmetic homework, consult on a proposed clothing purchase, mediate (or refuse to mediate) a squabble, and absorb enough of what my husband was telling me so that I'd know where to pick him up and when, all at the same time. I didn't always get it right in the beginning, and I still don't. I am, after all, the woman whose son told her in a moment of guileless affection, "I love you even if you forget things." But I find it strengthening to consider that maybe in a world of overwhelming problems, we women have something distinctive to offer from our experience of multiplicity. Down the centuries we have freed men from the web of domestic distraction so that they could concentrate on running the world. It would be gently, sweetly ironic if some of the skills they need turn out to be the ones we were learning at home.

We all have individual talents as well, of course. On bad days we might have to think quite a long time before we can remember any, and even on good days it is sometimes hard to tell yourself you are talented in needlework, for example, when without thinking you can name four other people who are more talented. Maybe we need to rethink another element of the world's system: competition. Logically we know that already. It is perfectly possible to be good at something without necessarily being better. If you enjoy needle-work (or art, or music, or whatever), if it gives you pleasure and you can take satisfaction in what you do with it, then it doesn't matter if other people can run circles around you. You're still talented. You would tell that to your children: remember to tell that to yourself.

In the final analysis, of course, what gives us the greatest confidence in our own value as ourselves is the knowledge that our spirits exist separate and free. They always have, and they always will. Nobody else's testimony can carry us closer to our Heavenly Father; nobody else's faults and misjudgments can stand in our way of returning to his presence. The magnificent riches of the scriptures and the words of the prophets were not given primarily to our husbands, leaving us to scavenge what we could, peering over their shoulders. Ultimately, each of us has a wholly independent relationship with the Lord. Ultimately, each of us will have to account for our time on this earth, to him, and to him alone. Whatever that account adds up to is the only certain measure of our value.

Perhaps the best thing to remember while we are moving on our way toward him is that we are creatures still in process, just as our children are, just as our husbands are. We are learning and ripening and stumbling along the path to wisdom and perfection, and some few golden days we get the whole formula right and a lot of ordinary gray days we don't. We were not sent out to be happy—we were sent out to learn joy, which is harder and more rewarding.

However insistently the world clutches at us, we are still ourselves, with our own choices to make, our own patterns to design on our own secret needles. We may drop stitches, we may miss rows—but through the slow labor of repentance we can go back and knit those places over, and we have been promised that the double-worked spots will not show. In the end the unique pattern that is the me in each of us will include all the rest of it: a husband's wife, the children's mother, and a daughter of God. In the end, if we have worked faithfully, honestly, and to the best of our infinitely various abilities, that unique pattern will be what we carry home—the only memento we can take with us for the next step in our great adventure.

CHAPTER 7

Bind Off: Cast On on New Needles

Nothing in mortality lasts forever. As unlikely as it may seem viewed from the perspective of days when there seem to be toddlers and babies as far as the eye can see and every single one needs a nose wiped or pants changed, the day does come when the children grow up and go away. The complicated, criss-crossing skein of family life unwinds, and there you are, with a set of empty needles. You did it. You taught them, and you coddled them, and you scolded them, and forever and always, you loved them, and now, just as you should be, you are redundant. They wipe their own noses, and they change their own pants; they make their own decisions and (hopefully) they earn their own livings.

It's the big change, the one you've always wondered if you'll be ready for.

The really curious part of the whole business is that

106

although I am watching my oldest daughters turn into adults before my eyes, I still don't feel, in spite of the years, that I've changed all that much myself. Oh, I'm occasionally somewhat taken aback by an unexpected sight of the face I see in a mirror, but inside it feels the same as it did the day I married or during all those years when I was pursuing them to wash their faces. Well, maybe not *exactly* the same — I hope I've learned something in the intervening period — but pretty close. Certainly I don't feel like a little old lady, which was what I had always assumed I'd be by the time the children finally started to move out on their own. Inside, I still feel the same as I've been all along, only maybe slightly astonished (after all those weeks that seemed to go on forever) that the whole child-raising process whipped by so quickly. But it did. As rapidly as they outgrew the sweaters I knit them, so am I apparently outgrowing the mother patterns I've been following all these years.

And what now? Here we are, the mothers of children on the brink of independence, discovering that we are ourselves on the brink of middle age (which requires its own quota of self-image adjustment), and trying to figure out where parenthood is taking us now. Some changes are positively encouraging. For one thing, there is the gratifying discovery that the children believe again that we know something. When they started out, they assumed we knew everything, in spite of all evidence to the contrary. By the time they reached adolescence, they were clearly aware of our inadequacies and convinced that anything we did know was

107

hopelessly out of date. Now, as they are beginning to encounter the complications of the real world for themselves, their view of us is edging back towards reality. They may not have gone so far as to consider us once again the fount of all wisdom, but at least now they are reassuringly confident that we aren't stupid. They even ask for advice sometimes, and on occasion, even more surprisingly, follow it.

There is also the delightful possibility that as our load of responsibility for our sons and daughters lessens, they become friends. Not friends like any of our ordinary, out-of-the-family friends, of course: the years have bound us together too tightly for that. When you've changed their diapers and tweezered splinters out of their fingers and consoled them when they weren't invited to the birthday party, common or garden-variety friendship, even after they've grown up, is no longer possible. You care too much about each other to permit such a tepid relationship. But a particularly individualized and personal friendship can flower, just because you do know each other so well. You know what makes them laugh; they know what tickles you. You can share family gossip without having to explain who everybody is. You may or may not share tastes in clothes or in entertainment, but even if there have been battles before, you're past that now, and you can enjoy your mutual agreement to disagree. And underneath the companionship that you might have had with anyone else, lies the devotion that belongs singularly to children and their parents. No one will ever love them as much; no one, except for themselves, will ever love their children as much.

But grandchildren are usually still well in the future when the children start to go. So where does that leave us as mothers now? Well, for once the good news and the bad news are exactly the same. The good news is that the children are going. Not going in the sense that you won't have anything more to do with them, but going in the sense that your twenty-four-hour-a-day stewardship is completed. If they stay out too late, you won't have to sit up waiting for them or try to sleep while listening to every car that passes the house. They may eat whatever bizarre items are on this week's diet, but since they aren't in your refrigerator, you won't have to know about it or worry about that either. You won't have to listen to their music unless you choose to or argue about the tidiness level in their rooms. (Ironically, once their turf is their own, they are likely to keep about the same level of cleanliness and tidiness that you do — and all those years you thought they never noticed!) Of course, you will all still be part of each other's lives. You'll see each other, if you're close enough, or talk (expensively) on the phone if you're not. But you will be free again, freer than you have been since you found out you were going to be a mother, all those years ago.

If the good news is that they are going, it's also the bad news. There is no dodging the unnerving reality that you will become less central to the flow of your children's lives. That's as it should be, as it must be, but it can leave an empty feeling until you get used to it. It's not just the house that will need reorganization. However ready you might have been for their departure, once they're gone, you have more to do than clean out bedrooms and decide what you are prepared to store indefinitely. You have to take a deep breath and recognize that your life has changed as irrevocably as it did when the first child arrived. Once again who you are is redefined.

When the children arrived, you changed from being one of a partnership of two to being the woman in the control booth, at least as far as the daily business of living went. You were the rememberer of details (which child needed which blanket to go to bed with, what year was the last tetanus immunization, who can drink milk and who can't). You were the primary scheduler, the food and nutrition specialist ("no, you may not have another cookie — it's only half an hour to dinner"). You were the one who could make whatever it was better, and the court of first resort to adjudicate fairness and determine whether the sweater in dispute was borrowed with permission or not. You were the one who decided which problems had to be referred to father. In many ways, you were the hub around which the individual spokes of the family rotated. Now the children are gone, and those jobs you have been doing for years no longer need to be done. Your place in the family has changed. You have to adjust yourself to no longer being the daily center of family life, as you adjust to setting fewer places at the table.

Filling up your time isn't usually the important problem. For most of us, time gets filled very easily.

It's what goes on inside our hearts and minds that is unsettling. The children have grown up, and they don't need us the way they did. Oh, sure, if we're lucky they would like to have us there to talk to and consult with, but their decisions are entirely in their own hands. Our opinions may be part of their decision-making process, but we are no longer indispensable. We have to learn not to need to be.

Fortunately, the adjustment doesn't have to be done all at once. As Latter-day Saint women, most of us have more children than our nonmember friends and neighbors do, which means that the child-leaving-home stage stretches out a lot longer. For some of us, the oldest child is heading off for college about the same time we are toilet-training the youngest. When that, or something close to it, is the chronology, it isn't quite the same as having the standard two children, spaced in the standard fashion, who depart within two years of each other. The mother of many, spread across many years, doesn't have the same sudden yawning emptiness. It's more like gently sliding off the edge of the cliff.

But whether it happens slowly, one by one, or all of a sudden, it happens. We have to readjust our sense of ourselves and refigure who we are. We necessarily assume a steadily diminishing role in the lives of our children, who are, as they should be, increasingly focusing on the next generation to come. One stage of our lives, the stage for which we prepared during all those years we coddled our dolls, draws to a close. And none of us did much rehearsing for whatever comes next.

Unfortunately, as a society we seem to assume that the transition should be an effortless one. To have a quiet weep as the overloaded car pulls away from the house (with madly waving hands visible above the heaped belongings), or as you drive away from the college dorm or the airport—that's okay. But you are expected to have your socks firmly pulled up the next day and be back to business as usual. Only wimps and maladjusted neurotics are expected to need a period of adjustment.

The trouble is that business as usual doesn't exist anymore. Our business was serving, providing continuous twenty-four-hour-a-day resources. We did it whether or not we had another job for which we received a paycheck. We did it well enough so that the children have developed resources of their own and the service isn't needed now, at least not in the same way. And whether they outgrow it all at once, or gradually over years during which the children one by one go off to school, to missions, to marriage, our own learning not to serve—or, more accurately, to serve differently—is a process that few of us experience without more distress than we are inclined to allow ourselves. We can fill up the hours of our day; we can go back to full-time employment, or start all over again on something new, but nothing else ever quite fills the space that mothering left behind. As we watch their strong, self-confident retreating backs, it's hard not to remember with wistful nostalgia when they were little and vulnerable and fit on our laps. Back in those days we may sometimes have longed for freedom. We are free now, but there are moments when we would trade that freedom for the remembered warmth of a small child's body, snuggling sleepily against us.

In some ways, the whole process of our children breaking away from us into their own lives is curiously analogous to labor. That was interesting, too; or it would have been if it hadn't hurt so much. In each case, we are integrally involved, and yet, oddly, spectators at the event. Halfway through labor, you can't suddenly decide you'd rather not do this today. If you panic and fight the contractions, you may be able to slow the process down somewhat, but that's about it. That mighty muscle, your uterus, is in charge, and it is way out of your conscious control. You are there, all right, but your body takes over and performs as it is programmed to do, whether you want to go along with it or not. In a somewhat similar way, your children will move into their own maturity with or without you. You can hang desperately onto their skirts, or the belt loops of their jeans, but all that will accomplish is to make the whole transition more difficult for everybody. Like your body, your children are already programmed to act. They may look back at you over their shoulders; with luck, they will always love and respect you, but that overwhelming and totally absorbing love you have always felt for them will, in their lives, be the love they feel for their children. Love flows downward through the generations, each repaying the last by the love they pour out on the next. Watching our children coping

113

with our grandchildren, seeing them try to control their exasperation with love just the way we always tried to do, is the only direct repayment we will ever receive — and all, really, that we want.

Watching them cope and keeping our opinions to ourselves, we still have lessons to learn, and that is one of them. At times the temptation to interrupt and pass on the wisdom we have so painfully gathered is almost irresistible, and yet learning to master that temptation is one more aspect of the self-control we were sent to this earth to achieve. Oh, there are indeed opportunities to share what we have learned, but those opportunities come primarily when we're asked for advice. The rest of the time we need to learn the lessons of "hands off," of love expressed by a willingness to let other people make their own mistakes, however clearly we could have pointed out the error of their ways, if only they had stopped and listened. And when the mistakes have been made and recognized, we learn to comfort them with the same patience we had when we comforted them back in grade school days, reassuring them that life is complicated enough so that everyone makes mistakes, and even parenting mistakes are survivable by parent and child alike. We can comfort and support, but this time the job is theirs. Our job is to move away from the center of the stage, hopefully with grace and voluntarily before we are nudged aside, even gently.

We have other fish to fry, in any case. There is no question that the children absorbed a major chunk of our time and attention, but except for the periods of really dire emergency (such as immediately after child-birth or when they all went down with chicken pox at once), there was always more going on in our lives than child-raising alone. Now, as the children depart and prepare to depart, we have more time and attention for the other things — our husbands, for example.

Back in the olden days (as the children used to describe any event that took place before they can remember), there were only two of us. Now we are only two again, and that old, pure relationship may need dusting off and refurbishing. For years the major proportion of husband/wife conversation has probably been directly or indirectly concerned with the children: endless discussion of transportation arrangements, rules, consequences for rule infractions, budgets, funny stories, worries, and mysteries never solved ("where do all those pairs of scissors and rolls of tape go?").

Nor was it only a matter of talking and thinking about the children. They were physically all over the place. When they were little, we had to keep stepping over them. As they grew older, they also grew bigger, and unless the house was really generously large, they were likely to careen into us absentmindedly going up and down the stairs and through the doorways. For years they followed us around like homing pigeons. The only times we could be confident of privacy were when they finally were all safely asleep, and even when we were reasonably sure they were, there was always the unnerving possibility of a small figure materializing unexpectedly at the side of the bed.

Going out presented its own complications. In the

early years, any plans for the two of us had to include babysitting provisions; later on, dinners or evenings out too often had to be tailored to accommodate dropping off or picking up offspring from the church or a friend's house or wherever else they happened to be. Later still, there was the question of who had which car when and was there any gas left in the car allocated for our use.

But now they are gone. The house is full of space and comfortable quiet. Now, once again, there is the delight of spontaneity. Now, once again, we can concentrate on each other. Feel like dinner out, just the two of us? It might have to be the local hamburger joint, since financial commitments to the children and their educations linger on after the children themselves are away, but there's no reason why we can't go out, just the two of us, and go back to the kind of two-person conversations that were part of courtship and early marriage. Only this time, out of all the years of shared living and experience, we have more to bring with us.

We know each other so well: we can communicate with the flick of a glance, a shrug, or a secret grin. We know what we can enjoy together, and what we have tacitly agreed, over the years, to enjoy separately. One of the joys of being old enough to have grown children is being old enough to know that there are a whole bunch of different ways to have a satisfactory marriage, and what suits the two of us is what is appropriate. By now, we should be able to enjoy what's good about our particular marriage, and tolerate or work to improve the rest, without the feeling that it has to fit into

116

anyone else's specification. We know too, with the acceptance of maturity, that we will not have forever on this earth together, and that we need to savor these years we do have, and prepare for the time we'll spend together during whatever comes next.

Nonetheless, we were certainly not intended to sit around with our hands folded, passively waiting. It's true that few of us may actively welcome the prospect of growing old, and all the florid advertising about the glories of the "golden years" (generally produced by developers of retirement communities and insurance companies) doesn't necessarily sound reassuring. Just the same, the Lord surely gave us these years for a purpose, and it is our business to figure out what that purpose might be. Perhaps our knitting is not entirely accomplished yet, and there are new patterns, new blessings to be discovered now that we have discharged most of the responsibilities that have kept us busy up until now.

One of the biggest luxuries is that there is more time. There is, finally, time to concentrate on enriching your singular, personal relationship with the Lord. *You* become one of those sisters sitting serenely in sacrament meeting, unencumbered and able to listen to the talks. (And since you have the possibility of that serenity every Sunday, eventually you will even be able to spend whole meetings corraling small energetic grandchildren and not mind at all!) You can read the scriptures and study the conference addresses when you feel like reading and studying—no longer do you have to grab whatever stray minutes come to hand. You have time to prepare Sunday School and Primary lessons, and time to pursue complicated genealogical research. Or maybe you'll be in a position to give yourself and the Lord a whole chunk of your time and go on a mission and discover for yourself the particular joy that lit up the letters your children wrote home from *their* missions.

You have time for yourself. You have less house-cleaning to do, for one thing, when there isn't a houseful of youngsters abandoning shoes and jackets all over the place, along with homework papers that will turn out to be vital tomorrow morning. You may well have a smaller house, or even the compact efficiency of an apartment, to keep up with. Rooms stay tidy, and the peanut butter fingermarks on the woodwork become a dimming memory. You can sleep late in the morning, if so inclined, and go to the bathroom without someone leaning on your knees or yelling complicated messages through the closed door. You can watch what you want to see on the television or argue companionably about it with your husband. You can turn on the ignition in the car without having your hearing damaged by the blast of high-volume hard rock because you forgot who was driving the car last.

You can go back and pick up the dropped stitches of the interests you had years ago that were swamped during the hectic activity of childraising or discover new ones you'd never thought about before or encountered wistfully when there wasn't a spare moment to pursue them. Sometimes you may have old friends to explore the new interests with, and other times the new interests bring new friends along with them. Sometimes it is most satisfactory to plug along on your own, rediscovering the quiet pleasure of solitude after all the crowded years.

It isn't the Garden of Eden, of course. We left there a very long time ago. There are frustrations and disappointments. Not all the children turn out exactly as we'd like them to be, and sometimes we can still admire and enjoy some of their accomplishments, and sometimes that may not be possible. As we get older, even faithful adherence to the Word of Wisdom is no guarantee of good health, and physical limitations do just that: they limit what is physically possible. Coping with your own infirmities, or those of your husband, can be hard. There is also the fact that statistically, women outlive men, and losing a husband creates an unmendable hole in a wife's life. It is not diminishing the comfort of knowing you will have eternity together to admit that you feel the searing emptiness of now. Oh, you'll go on, and there will be other good things that happen, but it won't be the same. But then, nothing ever is. When we came to this earth, we came to a life in which the only constant is change. Just as the seasons of the year swing past, year after year the same, and yet each spring, each winter different from the spring or winter before, so do we move through the seasons of our lives. We were little girls, then young women, then wives, then mothers. And then the children grew up, and so did we.

The years will grow swifter. In the quiet days that slip away, it may be hard to remember what was so difficult in the busy times. Fortunately, it is the good moments most of us tend to treasure: the summer days when the children ran to us in the sunshine, the winter evenings when we were cozy and together, the whole family safe and warm in the same room. For the sake of our daughters, let us vow to remember all of it, the good days and the frustrating, depressing days — to help, if we can, and to sympathize without patronizing when we can't. Whatever it was, it was life. It was our turn at mortality, our chance to learn what we could only learn here. What lessons come next, we can't know. We can only set our needles aside, and wait to find out.